The World of the Tarot

The World of the Tarot

The Gypsy Method of Reading the Tarot

Sergius Golowin

SAMUEL WEISER, INC.
York Beach, Maine

First published in German in 1983
as *Die Welt Des Tarot* by
Sphinx Verlag, Basel, Switzerland
© 1975 Sergius Golowin
© 1975, 1983 Sphinx Verlag, Basel

First published in English in 1988 by
Samuel Weiser, Inc.
Box 612
York Beach, Maine 03910

Library of Congress Cataloging in Publication Data
Golowin, Sergius
    The world of the tarot.

    Translation of: Die Welt des Tarot.
    Bibliography: p.
    Includes index.
    1. Tarot. I. Title.
BF1879.T2G6413 1988   133.3'2424   87–34100
ISBN 0–87728–642–6

Typeset in 12 point Caslon
Printed in the United States of America

Contents

About the Author

Sergius Golowin, born in 1930, learned a great deal about the Indian and European worlds of tarot and tantra from his parents, whose involvement with these topics was very extensive. He grew up in the half-slums of the Mattenhof quarter in Bern, an area which is today legendary. He met nomadic tribes, fortune tellers, theosophists and occultists there during his childhood. They had come to Switzerland as refugees to escape the totalitarian powers sweeping the continent.

After the Second World War, Golowin traveled through Europe and became interested in the mystery of tarot. He worked as a librarian from 1950 to 1968, and collected verbal reports about the Alpen cultures which had been forgotten in the whirlwind of the "economic miracle" (Wirtschaftswunder).

Today he is a freelance writer. In 1974, he received a prize from the Swiss Schiller Foundation for his "great service in the area of modern folklore and cultures on the 'fringes' of society."

About the Artist

Walter Wegmüller's clan traveled for centuries in the area between Emmental and Rüschegg, working as basket-makers, tinkers, and horse-dealers in the Bern area. Many of his ancestors were called upon by farmers to "i d'Joni luege" (read the cards) in the course of their acquaintance.

Walter Wegmüller, born in 1937, spent some time as a traveling street painter and maker of "jewelry that brings luck." He has recently been recognized as one of the founders of a new folk art, using the timeless symbols of the wandering folk (gypsies) and mountain herders to decorate clothing, furniture, and musical instruments.

His "Festival of the Lice-ridden Birds" in the Bern Matte in 1969, in which 1200 friends took part, was conceived as the beginning of a chain of "happenings" for a new feeling about life and a new type of art. Along with H. R. Giger and C. Sandoz, he is one of the foremost innovators of modern fantastical painting in Switzerland today.

About the Deck

The cards depicted in this book are known as the Gipsy Tarot Tsigane or the Zigeuner Tarot. Painted by Wegmüller between 1968–1974, the actual cards measured 2 3/4 x 4 1/4". The illustrations in the book are of the original Swiss deck. These same cards with the Major Arcana titled in both French and English are available from Samuel Weiser, Inc. They retail for $15.00.

Part One

THE WORLD OF THE GYPSIES

Chapter One

THE SAGA OF THE
GYPSY TAROT

THE TRUE ORIGINS OF the tarot are shrouded in mystery. During the Renaissance and Reformation, the great Theophrastus Paracelsus (1493–1541) wrote of images and figures that originated from the magical arts used by Babylonians and what he called heathens. He stressed that these images are often found in places where little attention is paid to them, but they are there for a reason if we could only recognize it. He mentioned images and figures found in old chapels, graves, in secret passages, and cliffs, or in uninhabited areas, and he believed there was much to be learned from them.[1]

Did he mean the ancient cave drawings which disciples of the magical arts of his time tried to interpret to learn the wisdom of the past? Or did he intend us to understand that the creators of those images were still alive, able to teach those who found them and wanted to learn? In any case, he wrote that the gypsies were well versed in the magical arts.[2] Wilhelm Postel, another great thinker in the realm of occult sciences, devised a key to some of the mysteries in the 16th century. He drew a mystical circle around which the letters T-A-R-O were written. Because they were in a circle, the letter T was both the beginning and the end of the word—tarot.[3]

In the beginning of the 17th century, a founder of the Rosicrucian Society mentioned in one of his works, "a book called T., which is, after the Bible, our highest treasure . . . . "[4] Is this holy work "T" perhaps the Tarot, as the heirs of the Rosicrucian teachings in the 19th and 20th centuries claim it to be? In his book about the Rosicrucians *(Rosicrucians, Their Customs and Secrets)*, H. Jennings writes of the "curious, dark, and in some ways barbaric 'arcana' of the Bohemians, Zingari, Gitanos and gypsies . . . the original, oldest revelation of God, surviving through all times."[5]

In *Heinrich von Ofterdingen*, a key book in Romanticism, the hero sees his entire past and future. "He was shocked, and thought he was dreaming, but when he looked again, he could no longer deny the resemblance. He could hardly believe his eyes as he saw, in a painting, the cave, the hermit and the old man next to him.. . . A number of figures he couldn't name, but they were familiar. He saw his own image in different situations. At the end he seemed to have become greater, more noble. The guitar rested in his arms, and the countess handed him a wreath. He saw himself at the imperial court, on a ship, in a close embrace with a slender, lovely girl, in a fight with wild looking men, and in friendly conversation with Saracens and Moors." Hermit and lovers, Emperor and priest, representations of the struggle against lower levels of consciousness in and around himself, etc. Using a little imagination, you can find all the elements of the tarot deck as it appeared in Novalis' day. And every good tarot reader still teaches that we see ourselves and the world—in fact, the entire game of life—as a reflection in the cards.

The writings of many great thinkers and poets seem to indicate that the tarot was an important element on the journey to discover the underlying essence of existence. Since the end of the 18th century, entire libraries have been written about the tarot. Learned people argue about the cards and how they are to be designed, interpreted and used, as well as where they originated. Occult societies have redesigned the cards to suit the ideas and tastes of their own groups.

J. A. Vaillant was, in the 19th century, one of the greatest researchers into the history of the gypsies. In his book *Histoire vraie des vrais Bohémiens (True history of the true Bohemians)*, he drew a comparison between the words "tarot" and "tantra." He believed "tarot" to be derived from ancient Hindi and gypsy tongues. Tantra is the school of Indian religion which seeks the secret of the divine in all manifestation through the use of mystical or magical ecstatic rituals. Although later researchers rejected his theory as overly imaginative, we must remember that his dictionary of the gypsy language is one of the most important reference books in modern study of the gypsies *(Grammaire, dialogues et vocabulaire de la langue des Bohémiens ou Cigain*, Paris 1868).

As early as the 18th century, the theory was propounded by Court de Gébelin that the four suits of the Minor Arcana corresponded to the suits (Varnas) of the original four castes in India. These were designed, not as a social pecking order, but as an expression of the various ways or paths to realizing the divine nature of human existence.

Figure 1. The system of the four elements (the seasons, the temperaments, etc.) as taught by Paracelsus and his disciple Thurneysser in Basel is basic to the tarot. Woodcut entitled "The Four Temperaments," from Leonhard Thurneysser, Quinta Essentia, *(Leipzig, E. Germany: Hans Steinmann, 1574), Vol. 8, Chapter 1, P. CL XII (Public Library of the University at Basel, Switzerland).*

In the 15th century, however, the Brahmans misused the concept of heredity to name themselves the highest caste, claiming the others were mere underlings, intellectually unfit to discuss matters of faith.[6] The nobles' caste had been weakened by internal squabbling over supremacy, and the Islamic and Tartar soldiers virtually wiped them out. Islamic rulers decried the worship of many gods, and schools of occult thought and their disciples were destroyed. Previously, in the 13th century, the great schools and centers of Tantra were destroyed, the people living there were slaughtered. Those who could, escaped to Nepal, Tibet, Assam, Burma, Southern India, Ceylon and Java. That was the end of the Golden Age of Tantra in India. Only in Tibet, Nepal and the Himalayan valleys did anything of the original traditions remain.[7]

The sagas of the gypsies' flight from the bloody, destructive Indian wars include tales of the families of once powerful Indian kings who hid among the gypsies to save themselves. Although for many years the Europeans looked down on them as descendants of the lowest rabble, at least some of the gypsies trace their ancestry back to the genuine Kshatriyas, Rajputs and other nobles.

After years of comparative study, J. Kochanowski wrote in his *Gypsy Studies* (New Delhi, 1963), "the more closely Indian people resemble the higher castes in New Delhi (Punjab Hindus and Rajput), the more they resemble the Romani gypsies of Europe. The closer a dialect is to Hindi-Rajastani, the closer it is to Romani, the language of European gypsies. The same is true of music, dance and other cultural expression."

C. G. Leland, one of the greatest modern experts in the field of gypsy and witch cults and traditions, cites the 17th century inquisitor De Lancre, who compared the activities of sorceresses with the customs of secret Asian

Ces pauures gueux pleins de bonadue͞tures
Ne portent, rien que des Choses futures.

Figure 2. Mass migrations from mysterious Asia, like that of the Gypsies, were always a prelude to cultural transformation. Engraving entitled "The Gypsies on their Way," by Jacques Callot, from a catalog of his engravings edited by J. Lieure (Paris, 1924), p. 374.

cults. He said that a dance of naked Persian girls was comparable to a European witches' sabbath, and that their music was similar as well. Leland also mentions that magic, beautiful dancers, and mysterious sorcerers were part of the German Middle Ages. These people always appeared to be from the East, which indicates that long before the 15th century, tribes from India reached Europe and began spreading the teachings of Shakti and Tantra.[8] This might explain the great gypsy migration which reached Europe in the late 14th and early 15th centuries. Can it be mere coincidence that, at the same time, a wave of interest in the occult swept Europe? Artistically sophisticated tarot cards were designed for the nobility to use in divination. Perhaps they were brought to Europe by the gypsies.

When the Indian nobles were driven from their homes by bloody wars for supremacy, they were forced to go into hiding, which, as we mentioned, many did by joining groups that traveled from court to court, festival to festival as musicians, dancers, entertainers and magicians. The priests had labeled these people godless, and stripped them of their rights. In order to escape persecution, they began to wander from land to land, disseminating the true spirit of Indian culture wherever they went. From behind the mask of carnival entertainment, they spread invaluable, timeless wisdom. In Samarkand, Bagdhad, Astrachan and Krakau, schools of mysticism and the occult sciences blossomed.

One of the most striking resemblances between gypsy and Indian culture is that of language. In the letters T-A-R-O, we can see a rearrangement of the syllables RO-TA, or wheel. (Note: The German word for wheel is "Rad.") The Swiss gypsies call their wagons "Rotel,"[9] and "rotla" means to drive or travel. This, incidentally, is why Walter Wegmüller drew two wheels at the bottom of each card in his deck.

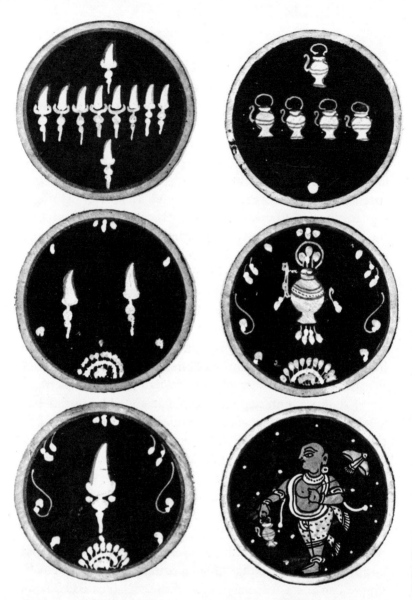

Figure 3. The symbols and numerology of the Indian game about the physical manifestations of the gods (called Deva-vatara), and those of the tarot, suggest that the two have common origins. Illustration of the Deva-vatara game is mid-20th century India, and is from the private collection of Walter Wegmüller.

They can be seen as wheels of fortune, but are intended to honor the old tarot masters–the gypsies from all tribes.

In the end of the 14th century, some people were convinced that the tarot cards were of oriental "Saracen" origin. The cards at that time were called "Naib" (Naipes).[10] Two centuries ago, Breitkopf sought the explanation for this name in the Arabic "nabi," a word meaning prophet, seer, soothsayer. Chatto[11] thought of the Hindi "naib," the word for an administrator of a district. Others looked to the Sanskrit "nabhi," meaning race or family. In the Indian-Tibetan occult sciences, the word for the area of the body which roughly corresponds to what we call the solar plexus is "Nabhi-Padma."[12] Nabhi (navel) virtually means middle, midpoint, or, the "navel" of the wheel,[13] which brings us back to RO-TA.

Attempts have been made to link the word "tarot" to the name of a Tibetan diety, Tara (star), an embodiment of eternal wisdom. The Sanskrit root "tar" in Avatar (a manifestation of Vishnu in human form) means to travel an ocean to its very end, to master it completely. The ocean is, of course, a symbol for this world of eternal change.

Writing about Indian gods, W. Eidlitz *(Die indische Gottesliebe)* wrote that Tara is also a name of Vishnu, meaning Brahma in his unmanifest form, as well as the sound "Aum" from which all is manifest. The substantive "taro" means raft, boot or ferry. Taro, or Tarota, as some students of the occult sciences write it (also Taro-Rota), is the wheel or cycle of divine symbols which help the person contemplating it find the meaning of existence or creation, according to Eidlitz.

The Italian Colocci, writing in 1880 about the gypsies *(Gli Zingari)*, pointed out that the gypsies were convinced they had known the cards since their conception, and that they gave the four suits, "colors," names which, to some

A'DDA-NARI

Figure 4. In the 19th century, re-discoverers of European magic found inspiration for the tarot card "the World" in Indian representations of the eternal divine cycle of creation. Notice in the Indian symbol that the four suits of the tarot are found in the four hands of Addi-Nari. Illustration from Transcendental Magic, *by Eliphas Levi (York Beach, ME: Samuel Weiser, 1970), p. 162.*

extent, seem to derive from Indian dialects. The name "spathi" supposedly derives from the Sanskrit "sa-patri" meaning "having leaves." "Pal" came from "pallav" meaning a branch with leaves. "Rup" comes from the Hindustani word for money, "rupee," and "pohara" seems to derive from the Hungarian word for cup.

The gypsies in Switzerland today call all playing cards (but especially those used for divination) "joni." The "j" is pronounced like the English "y." The Vedic word yoni originally meant path, resting place, seat.[14] Over the ages, this word took on such meanings as source, womb, birth, clan, caste, race, homeland, life, lifetime, body (as the container of the soul), etc.[15] The root means "to set in motion."[16]

Myths and symbols also seem to bear similarities in both cultures. Many people knowledgeable in the magic of Europe and Asia believe that the gypsy clans, moving from India to Europe, brought with them the ancient mystical symbols which are the keys to the original myths of humanity. In the late 18th century, Breitkopf said that the idols seen in the homes of German and Russian gypsies were similar to those used by the Kalmucks (Mongols).[17]

Amulets have been used by gypsies in Europe, in the Ural region, and on the Persian border. The myths associated with the amulets contained Indian imagery and gods, such as Laki (Lakshmi), Yandra (Indra), etc. In one image, a snake coils around a radiant star, which represents the original deity Baramy (Brahma).[18]

The huts and wagons of the gypsies sometimes contain modern pictures of Indian deities like those found in the markets of India. The gypsies claim they are similar to the ones that hung many years ago in gypsy dwellings. One reliable witness[19] related having seen very un-Christian looking icons in Carpathian gypsy wagons when he was a child at the turn of the century. One icon depicted a

Figure 5. The custom of "i d'Joni luege" (gazing into the cards) practiced by wise women has changed very little over the centuries. Illustration entitled "The Card Reader" is a 19th century German copper engraving.

very dark-skinned Christ-child in the protective coils of a many-headed snake. Paintings he saw later of the child-god Krishna reminded him of the icon he saw as a child. Did the gypsies adopt these symbols from other groups while traveling from Asia, or did they themselves bring the religious images from India?

A very popular Indian myth tells of a weaver who lies dying because he is hopelessly in love with the daughter of a powerful king. A friend consoles him by saying anything can be achieved through the four means. These are roughly translated as medicinal plants, money, powerful magical incantations, and human cleverness. The friend, skilled in the magical arts, then makes a small wooden flying machine in which the weaver can fly to the highest story of the seven (!) story palace where the princess is sleeping. He boldly claims to be Vishnu, and demands her hand in marriage according to the laws of the fairy folk. In order to convince her to acquiesce, he tells her she was, in an earlier life, Radha, the cow herder who married Krishna (Vishnu in human form). The queen overhears them and tells the king about the miracle. He is so thrilled by his close relationship to a deity that he begins to overextend himself and, as a result, loses a war with a neighboring kingdom. His enemies imprison him in the castle. The weaver realizes the consequences of his actions, and decides not to desert his beloved to save himself. He leads the weakened troops of the king as they set out for their final battle. They are hopelessly outnumbered and he realizes that the enemy will not fall for his ruse; he will make an easy target for enemy arrows. The great Naranjana, or Vishnu, is amused by the mess. He knows that the weaver is acting out of infinite love, trying to behave nobly in a desperate situation. Vishnu causes his own steed–the magical eagle Garuda–to enter the weaver's poor machine, while Vishnu himself enters the body of the forlorn weaver. The glory of the divine radiates from the

Figure 6. Icons offered at the marketplaces in India and imported by the hippies in the late sixties to Europe and North America are reminiscent of tarot art. Here we see a popular traditional Indian icon of the mid-20th century.

young man, and the battle is easily won. Everyone knows that the weaver is a mere mortal, but because he is able, if only for a moment, to become one with the divine, the King allows him to marry the princess.[20]

This myth is not a product of the medieval Indian priesthood. It seems much more to be the product of the philosophical nobles and their entertainers – or, if you will, the original gypsies. The story begins, as do so many modern-day gypsy stories, in the midst of a folk festival. We needn't be surprised, then, to find the entire story of "The Weaver as Vishnu" told almost exactly the same way among European gypsies. It was first written down by Wlislocki[21] and variations were made so the story would not be blasphemous to Christian hearers, but otherwise, it is the same. In Europe the young man is a noble, not a weaver. He is a happy young man whose heart is always open to the wandering folk (gypsies). Because of his generosity, he receives divine rewards despite the lies he tells (all inspired by love, of course).

The European story begins, "In a land where it is always summer (!) there lived a young man who was good to everyone. He was very rich, and any poor person who came to him received food, drink, money, and beautiful clothes." When he selflessly helps an old beggar, the beggar reveals himself to be Saint Nicholas and builds the young man a wooden bird that flies. The man then flies over the "seven high walls" to find the king's beautiful daughter. He tells her he is "the son of the dear God." The king is proud of his divine connections, but envious people try to unmask the young lover as a fraud and also try to kill him. Saint Nicholas reappears to explain that it is "the wish of our dear God" that the young man marry the princess.

The Eastern European gypsies also speak of four "means," although not necessarily in connection with this

Figure 7. The myth of Vishnu's magical eagle, Garuda, and the original tarot images both traveled from East to West. This illustration of the magical bird Garuda, with Vishnu (Krishna) and Lakshmi (Radha) is 18th century, from India or Pakistan. From the Islamic Museum, Berlin.

story. I first heard these mentioned by my father (who heard them from his father) and by Albert Minder (1879–1965) who was descended from the Jena gypsies, and who chronicled the history of the Swiss gypsies. The four means are power, money, magical skills and wise speech.

In another fairy tale told by the Czech gypsies, the hero, Kalo Dant, travels through the seven worlds, becomes rich and powerful, and even wins the heart of the great chief's daughter.[22] Gypsies often call themselves "The Black Ones," but Kalo Dant is called "The Black One with Teeth." This refers to the folk saying, "Magicians are born with teeth."

In order to become a magician, a person needed to be daring and enthusiastic, as well as knowledgeable and experienced. In other words, both young and old. A magician gained knowledge and experience through living–at least long enough to have a full set of teeth, including the well-named wisdom teeth–and had to retain the energy and enthusiasm of youth. Someone who had begun to lose teeth would be too old and would have lost the youthful enthusiasm and curiosity necessary. Conversely, an energetic, but inexperienced, person "without teeth" would be unable to fill the magician's shoes.

Everywhere gypsies have traveled, settled and lived for a while, people have had mixed reactions to them. The gypsies have been greatly valued, held in awe, feared and hated. People have tried to force them to settle down and give up or give away their secret knowledge. They have been honored by some, persecuted by some, and exterminated by still others.

The Tartar conqueror, Timur Lenk, called the gypsies a rebellious tribe and sought to exterminate them, but in Eastern Europe, they held, at least for a while, honored

Figure 8. Ever since the Middle Ages, European persecutors of the "wandering" clans have tried to snatch away from them the wisdom they have faithfully preserved over the centuries. Etching by Pierre Morel entitled "The Girl at the Ourse," Paris, 1888.

places in society. Nobles throughout Eastern Europe at the time of the czars enjoyed the music, dance, entertainment (and women) of the gypsies. The gypsies knew "their" nobles well and were an integral part of court life. These nobles were overthrown and are long dead, but their gypsies survive.

In some parts of Europe, gypsies were tortured to force them to give up secret knowledge people believed they had—such as how to use herbs to prolong life. But the most horrible and effective attempt to exterminate them was carried out by the fascists between 1933 and 1945. The bloodiest time of persecution began in 1939 with a law which sent all gypsy (and German) card readers, palm readers or practitioners of other arts of divination to concentration camps. Some believed it was envy which led Hitler to persecute the gypsies—he wanted his "Master race" to be the only one to be privy to the ancient Aryan wisdom of occult practices and mysteries. According to one story, a gypsy chieftain or a wise woman is supposed to have told him, "Your star will pale and you will perish in fire." Whether we choose to believe this story or not, the gypsies survived; Hitler's realm did not.

Wherever they were forced to go through the ages, the gypsies retained their own language, beliefs and customs. They held together, remembering that family and clan were their most precious possessions, so moving and upheaval were never a catastrophe. An old Russian gypsy I met in 1947 told me he had traveled with his clan from Siberia through Persia, Syria, North Africa, Spain, and then to France as a result of the Russian Revolution of 1917–1921. He said that for most people, such a trek meant the crumbling of their world. Their temples were burned, their rulers in flight, their soldiers either turned coward, traitor or pillager. Their money was worthless and the crops destroyed.

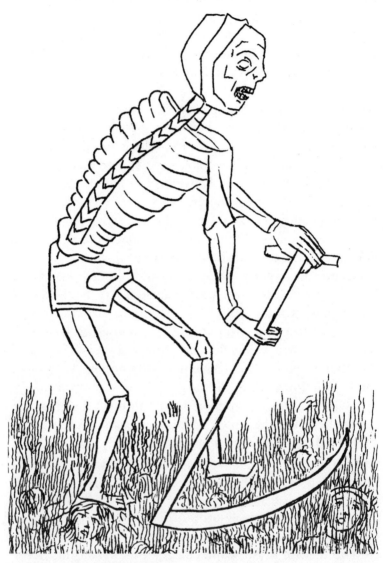

Figure 9. According to our ancient divination tradition, Death is a means or removing the used, the wilted, or the old to make way for new life, new Spring. Illustration from The Primitive World, *by Court de Gebelin, Vol. 8, Paris, 1781.*

But all these horrors were nothing compared to what evil people did to each other when they lost faith in their gods, and felt themselves forsaken. The gypsies believe that when you lose your faith, you lose everything.

In their travels throughout the world, the gypsies have seen many rulers come and go, many wars, and many lands change hands. They know that The Tower, held upside down, shows two people dancing above it all, above the destruction all around them. This understanding, their deep connection to their ancestors, and their experience of wandering through the ages helped the gypsies relocate after World War II, as well.

While many Europeans sat despairing on the rubble heaps, gypsies were hard at work making a life for themselves again. Their skills as smiths and mechanics helped them put wrecked cars back on the road and fix all sorts of machinery. Their ability to learn languages quickly helped them act as interpreters for both Russians and Americans. Their knowledge of herbal lore helped them turn meagre rations into nutritious repasts using roots, seeds and berries. The gypsies knew the importance of helping each other. The true gypsy always sets his or her talents and resources at the service of the clan.

Most importantly, perhaps, the gypsies read the cards. They understood that the surrounding desolation and destruction carried the seeds of rebirth, so they gave many despairing people hope, assuring them that conditions were bound to improve.

The gypsies understand well—because of centuries spent observing many cultures—the cycle of life. The people who are in power will eventually fall, those who are down-trodden will eventually rise—the first will be last and the last will be first. The tarot is the great calendar of Life. It shows us that each of the four suits comes and goes in turn. Some people will feel most comfortable and move

Figure 10. In the markets of the old cities, ancient tradition meets youth seeking spiritual adventure. Photograph by Dieter Hagenbach: "Marit in Bern."

most easily through a coins time, such as we have today, particularly in America, Western Europe and Japan. Those who are uncomfortable in the time of coins can be comforted in the knowledge that the elements change places as surely as the seasons. Someone who loves summer has to acknowledge and accept the coming of autumn, when other people will enjoy their peaks. And the passing of each day brings the next summer closer.

We can see this law demonstrated as every generation grows up. Children find their parents' values and gods disappointing, and look to the past for inspiration and guidance. The elements shift balance as each generation matures and imposes its own re-discovered values on the world. After generations of ridicule and persecution, gypsies are again sought for their knowledge of folk arts and divination. According to one report, police in Paris estimate that 300,000 people go to professional card readers and other people skilled in divination *every day!* Many of the young people involved in these arts claim to have gypsy blood. A Swiss religious underground newspaper in Zurich *(Religion im Untergrund)* described a hippie community in the Swiss Alps in 1975. "No wood is to be found. An occasional blueberry bush grows underfoot. Twelve huts with stone walls and plastic roofs, a cooking hut, six small tents and two large ones stand there. Near the buildings, stones mark out a circle on the ground, where the camp meets to eat, talk, and to play the great game, tarot."

A successful book (and movie) of that era, *Dr. Terror's House of Horrors,*[23] says of the tarot, "This card game is a picture book of life, an answer to questions of history and philosophy, the most basic questions of all. And sometimes, sometimes it is a means of prophecy."

Numerology and the Tarot

Almost more important than the 4, the numbers 1–10 and 22 in the tarot, is the number 7. The number of Minor Arcana, 56 (8 x 7) was important in old Rosicrucian scriptures. If we divide the cards into male (Wands, Swords) and female (Coins, Cups), each division contains 28 cards, the number of days in a lunar month.

Since the Fool (card 22) usually carries the number 0, it has often been omitted from the Major Arcana, leaving 21 cards in the Major Arcana and 77 in the entire deck. These are 3 and 11 times 7. Already in the 18th century, in his history of German Freemasons, E. Servati wrote that certain wise men called Freemasons treasured the secret fact that the tarok (sic) was based on the sacred number 7.

The holiness of the number 7 was also treasured by Madame Blavatsky. Did she assume this knowledge from the ancient traditions of India during her travels there, as she claimed? Or did she learn it from the tarot cards first, which she considered to be the illustration of the oldest myths of the world? (She found the decks used for divination at her time too distorted to be useful for her purposes.)[24]

For Blavatsky and her followers, the number 7 indicated the number of steps to development of the consciousness. In fact, most modern occult schools of thought speak of 7 worlds, or 7 levels of consciousness,[25] or mention the number 7 in some way. Seven is the number of days in the week, which corresponded to the 7 planets which ancient astrologers were able to see. Followers of Vishnu say each of these planets is a radiation of a basic energy of Vishnu. In India the number 7 plays an enormous role in history (which involves an almost unimaginable number of years).

Each creation day of Brahma has 14 divine law givers (Manus). During the period one is active, there are 7 great seers (Rishis) who also can appear as ancestral gods, and, along with their wives, form another circle of 14 divine beings.[26]

In another ancient Indian model which is also a basic symbol in Tibetan Buddhism, the holy Mount Meru stands in the center of the world; 28 heavens rise above it, and 7 rings of mountains stand around it. There are also the four directions, each containing one major continent and two minor continents. Each of these sections corresponds with one side of the holy mountain. The four directions, of course, are related to the four basic elements of creation, and the four divine rulers of the four regions of the world. They are the East, the sunrise; the thrower of lightning bolts, Indra; the South, the fire god Agni; the West, the water god Varuna; the North, Kubera, the god who rules all earthly riches.

We can also see in the cards a representation of the four seasons. A Parisian reader added his own concept to this theory: he saw the 4 times 14 cards as an expression of the 52 weeks of the year. Probably in accordance with an old tradition, he combined the king and queen as a pair to represent the end of each season. Each pair stood for either a solstice or an equinox.

If we continue along these lines, the four sets of fourteen cards become sets of thirteen, which gives us not only the number of weeks in the years, but also is four times the number sacred to sun cults, and the number of the lunar months in the year. Thirteen is also the number of signs in the zodiac, the thirteenth being the sun god who stands at the center of the circle of twelve moon gods.

Part Two

THE MEANINGS
OF THE CARDS

Chapter Two

THE WANDS

A T ONE POINT IN INDIAN history, some power-hungry
priests and rulers turned the caste system into a ladder-
like system with themselves at the top, but the original
system was a wheel with four spokes. The four castes correspond to the four elements (fire, earth, air, water) whose
interaction create the material world. The castes are four
possible ways of discovering the divine in all things and
expressing it in our daily lives. They should check and
balance each other so that none dominates.[1]

The original order of the castes started with the club,[2]
also called a cudgel, stick, rod, or wand. The image is
clear—a branch, stick or tree trunk served ancient people
both as a tool and as a weapon. A French tarot reader once

told me, "The stick is the arm of the masses," a neat play on words. A sword in the hand of a master fencer is dangerous, but clubs in the hands of a dissatisfied, anonymous majority are unconquerable.

This fact may have some relation to the words used to describe ancient societies. In the 18th century attempts were made to correlate the name of the English Freemasons with the word for club (Masue), just as the word for a group of people with common interests (club) seems to derive from the word for the "people's arm." In Wallis, in the Swiss Alps, the people gather around the Mazze, a staff with a history associated with magic, whenever they want to band together to fight an injustice which effects them as a group.

In those times, the power of the masses was so great that the nobles could rule only as long as they kept aware of the mood of the people. As long as justice was assured, and the lords were generous in providing amusement at festival times, the nobles were safe. But if they felt it was beneath them to keep abreast of the situation among their people, their mistakes in ruling would weld the people together until they arose as a single club, to strike down the offenders, whose weapons were powerless to defend them.

The tarot readers I spoke with in many parts of Europe echoed the age-old idea that politicians concerned about their success must look to the people. The Wands always indicate what influences are at work in relation to the people in your environment.

If you let your imagination wander freely, you may be able to associate many things with sticks, rods, clubs or wands. Bound together in a row, sticks can form a fence—protection from wild animals or human intruders. If you substitute the common people for sticks, they represent unity, an invincible defense.

The Wands represent forces for growth. They are the only suit in the tarot which is an object found in nature. Some tarot decks show the wands covered with buds or flames. Thousands of years ago, a stick was used to make holes in the ground to plant seeds. The first plows were wooden. Sticks were used to herd cattle, and divining rods helped people find water. Mines cannot be dug without wooden supports to reinforce the walls. Sometimes, in some decks, the wood is combined with metal so the wands depict lances, axes, picks, shovels or hammers. They represent the abundant and varied tools we have developed over the ages to better deal with nature.

This first suit represents the first caste, all people who use their bodies to reap nature's bounty and make the products into objects useful to humanity. They are the farmers, miners and loggers, and the people who work in factories. The Wands person works directly with visible matter, and is in touch with the divine nature of existence through observing nature's cycle of growth and death. This can lead to a deep understanding of life and growth as a miracle, but it may also lead to materialism, the superstition that matter is all there is and that only the masses, the majority, are right.

Life is most meaningful for Wands people when they remain aware of the intrinsic value of their unity. If they forget the spirit of working together, they become a grey, anonymous, uncaring mob, and can easily be manipulated by others. They become a club in the hands of factions with more political power, and are used to fight out all political and religious wars.

On the Magician card the carnival entertainer has the symbols of the three other castes on the table before him, but the wand is in his hand, raised above the others. The wand will make his performance of magic and transformation possible.

Page of Wands

Meaning: You receive good news from the realm of Wands.

Inverted: You receive bad news from the realm of Wands.

The page is a messenger, a helpful soul who brings news from his realm. He may represent information received from the media which, when properly understood and implemented, will help you reach your goal. He may also symbolize a guest or a new acquaintance whose conversation or behavior contains important lessons for you.

Some tarot readers see the pages or knaves as feminine figures. In some decks, they are, in fact, depicted as princesses. They can also indicate a meeting with a woman who will help you progress in her realm.

Knight of Wands

Meaning: You receive support from the young people of the world of Wands. Whether your undertaking concerns the realm of Wands, Coins, Swords or Cups, this card promises you will enjoy the whole-hearted support of enthusiastic people.

Inverted: The chances are that the people around you (workers and friends) will leave you, or that the life forces which vitalized you at the outset of your undertaking will slowly "ride away" and be lost.

RITTER-STAB

Queen of Wands

Meaning: You receive beneficial support from a Wands-type woman.

Inverted: You are subject to difficulties from or with such a woman.

The Queen of Wands is also called the Queen of Fire. She is queen over the fire spirits (which, in accordance with Paracelsus, are still often called salamanders or vulcans). She is an adult with a fixed social position, is usually married, and always has dealings with natural growth, farming, and work with the elements of the earth. She is occasionally the woman who chooses to live in the country, or she is remarkably practical, understanding a great deal about farming, gardening and handicrafts.

King of Wands

Meaning: You will benefit from the friendship or loyalty of a man like the King of Wands.

Inverted: You are subject to the enmity of such a man, or will fail to receive his assistance when you most need it.

The King of Wands is also called the King of Fire, and is the king over fire spirits. He is a strong, manly, active, Mars-like man, whose work centers on growth and the earth element. His outstanding characteristic is a wealth of vital forces—an almost contagious good health.

Ace of Wands

Meaning: The fire of creativity, an abundance of natural energies and the resultant joy in existence are all yours. You have everything you need, all the vital forces required, to begin a project or continue one successfully.

Inverted: You can sink into an uncreative state because you fail to recognize your own basic talents and gifts.

The interpretation of the numbered cards in the tarot closely follows the science of numerology as it has been taught for over a century by occultists in the West. The science stems in a large part from the gypsy-researcher Vaillant[3] and is mentioned extensively in the works of Gérard Encausse (1865–1916), who founded various esoteric circles among the nobles in the court of the last Czar. Many modern occult or magic societies date back to those groups.[4]

Vaillant's numerology is based on secret teachings of the oldest Himalayan tribes which have been best preserved by the gypsies. The ace, or the number 1, for example, represents the undivided oneness, the whole not yet split into dualities, the circle of all possibilities in the Universe, the eternity of time and the endlessness of space.

Two of Wands

Meaning: Your energies (the fire in the blood) are depleted, but this is only a natural ebb which will soon give way to a new influx of energy.

Inverted: The depletion of your energies can easily lead to your subjection or enslavement to someone who is stronger.

The number 2 represents branching out. It symbolizes two poles, the original duality which is the wellspring of all manifestations. It is the above and below, masculine and feminine, fire and water, light and shadow, sun and moon, joy and sorrow. This is also the realm of paradise and hell, immortal heroes and mere human beings, Suras (gods) and Asuras (demons) in Indian mythology.

Three of Wands

Meaning: You become able to emerge from conflict the victor.

Inverted: Your will is crippled. You feel discouraged and exhausted.

According to the "Indian-gypsy" teachings of 19th century occultists, three is the annulment of the original duality, the tension between sun and moon, male and female, spirit and matter, or light and dark. The third point creates a new dimension, a triangle, and with it, the space for establishing balance between the poles.

The number 3 symbolizes the sidereal zone which, with the sun and moon, forms the trinity (trimurti). We find the trinity in many ancient religions. The Indians know it as Brahma the Creator, Shiva the Destroyer, and Vishnu the Preserver.

Four of Wands

Meaning: People around you whose attitudes and concepts are different from yours gain vitality and start to resist you in some way. They may be neighbors, coworkers, family members, etc.

Inverted: Your vitality is exhausted because you come into conflict with laws of reality which you do not fully understand.

The number 4 symbolizes the visible world which is brought about by the trinity's eternal cycle of creation, preservation, and destruction. We have four seasons, four directions, two pairs of solstices and equinoxes, four weeks of the month, four elements, and the cross which can be formed when you spread out your arms.

Brahma, the god of creation, possesses four heads. In a fable, he tells his wife Saraswati, "I want to be able to see you from four sides," meaning seeing and judging from all possible different perspectives.

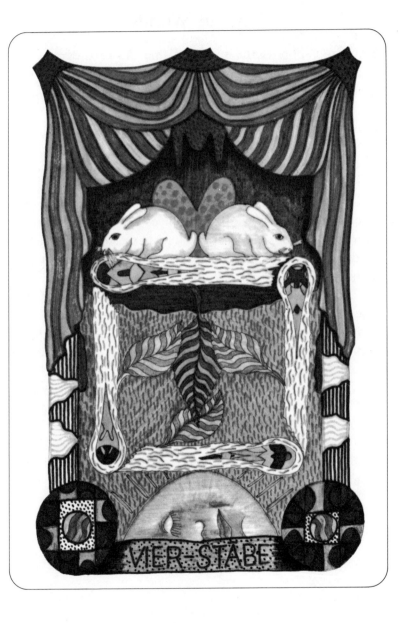

Five of Wands

Meaning: This is the blazing flame. You experience an increase and concentration of your energies. Success and good health are yours!

Inverted: Defeat and illness plague you.

Five represents the five planets visible to the naked eye, the five senses, the five elements of ancient Indian philosophy, and the five heads of Shiva. The trinity represented the resolution of duality, and five resolves the conflict between all four apparently opposed elements—seasons, personality types, etc. The integrated interaction of these different elements gives rise to the abundant variety of our world.

Four of Shiva's heads represent elements. Prithivi represents earth, Jala represents water, Agni represents fire, and Vajyu represents air. The fifth head, Akasha, usually is depicted as rising above the others. It represents what is usually translated as ether—the divine force in, behind and above all manifestations. Only one who knows the origins and effects of ether can begin to see the essence of the world.

This is the significance of the number five in nearly all magical traditions. It is often depicted as a five-pointed star, a pentagram, the seal of Solomon, or a Druid's foot.

Six of Wands

Meaning: You are dancing in the electrical field of sensory passions. This may develop into a bustle of activity which, in the end, can be seen as senseless.

Inverted: You are in a chaos of passions. This state often involves disappointment, disillusionment, disloyalty and betrayal.

Occultists see the number 6 as opposition which arises from doubling the trinity. The year has an "ascending" and a "descending" half, each of which is divided into three parts. The result is six periods of two months each, so each half-year has a beginning, a middle and an end, or declining portion.

The Hindu trinity of Brahma, Shiva and Vishnu is almost always represented as a circle with six figures. Each of the gods has his female aspect, his "wife," one of the major goddesses. This corresponds to the idea of the six days of creation, during which each of the gods in turn creates, preserves, and destroys the world in a never-ending cycle.

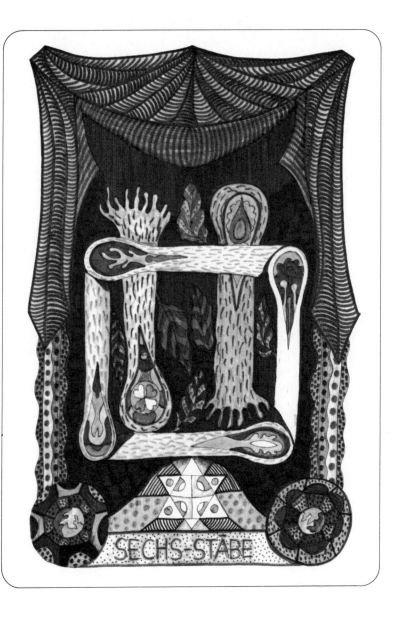

SECHS-STÄBE

Seven of Wands

Meaning: Your knowledge and mastery of life forces increase, assuring success in all areas of your life.

Inverted: You are uncertain of your powers because you repeatedly fail to recognize their nature and their source.

The sun gods Apollo (Greek) and Suriya (Indian) each have seven steeds. The seventh day, Sun-day, was always, surely even in ancient cultures, a day for rest and contemplation. It has always been a day to regard the world as a tremendous work of art in which all is held in balance. The new arises from the ashes of the old, and every resting period is followed by an awakening to new clarity and realization.

The number 7 symbolizes the seven stars of the poles, as well as the seven sidereal nights of the lunar month when the moon doesn't shine. Gypsies believe these nights give birth to the seven days of the week. We can also see the trinity in the waxing, full, and waning moon, giving us three times seven, the number of moonlit nights, and of the cards in the Major Arcana.

Eight of Wands

Meaning: The development of your energies is at a standstill. You consider the seeming contrast between your own potential and the energies of the outside world working against you.

Inverted: You are at a standstill, confused, disappointed. Gloomy, discouraging thoughts—even thoughts of death—occupy your mind.

Symbols for duality abound on this card—above (divine) versus below (earthly, material), inner versus outer, etc. When we are lost in the world of illusion, we tend to see these as opposing, warring elements.

A Parisian occultist told me the eight is an excellent symbol for eternity. The two circles which form the number can be drawn either one atop the other, or side by side. They actually represent two magic mirrors, like the ones we sometimes see in gypsy wagons. They hang opposite each other, endlessly throwing the light, the same image, back and forth. Eight symbolizes the consciousness caught in the cycle of birth and death. This cycle remains unbroken until the great oneness is realized and the inner and outer worlds are recognized as the divine merely throwing its own image back and forth.

Nine of Wands

Meaning: You are filled with renewed energies, physical strength, good health and overflowing joy in existence.

Inverted: You experience failure due to exhaustion. You are despondent in the face of relatively insignificant opposition.

Nine is the number of renewal, or cosmic, as well as human, pregnancy. In ancient times, people celebrated the spring equinox as the end of winter's night and the rebirth of the sun and earth. It was seen as the new marriage of the divine, which filled the earth, the world, nature with its potent energies and vital forces, making everything fruitful.

Nine months later, at the time of the sacred mid-winter when the powers of darkness seem to conquer everything, the new sun-god, liberator of all beings, was thought to be reborn to begin his inexorable triumphal march. The Indian myth of the liberator Krishna (the human manifestation of Vishnu) might have been the original representation of this process. Krishna was born of the goddess Devaki—at a time when powerful and evil oppressors ruled—and brought love and joy to all beings. Nomads from India spread this and other wonderful sagas throughout all lands, creating a basis for the remarkable resemblance of legends and sacred images in so many of the world's religions.

Ten of Wands

Meaning: You have a calm awareness of all your powers, accomplishments, and abilities – the best basis for constant success. This card indicates continual forward progress.

Inverted: Inverted, the Ten of Wands indicates the reduction of life-energy, sterility, or fruitlessness.

Ten is a new oneness. It is the number 1 that occurs after a completed cycle, as some occultists see it as zero. This oneness is attained after journeying through and overcoming a confusing multitude of possibilities. This is the moment in which the reborn consciousness learns to see the ultimate oneness of all things behind the multiplicity – the entire play of mind and the world.

A card reader convinced me that 10 is the direct outcome of renewal (the number 9) by pointing out an ancient train of reasoning. She said that birth (this completion and this eternal earthly new beginning) requires nine solar months which are, simultaneously, ten lunar months of 4 weeks, or 28 days!

It has been said that in the Himalayan cultures an age is complete when Vishnu has appeared ten times in mortal form to help humanity keep from the despair of life's difficulties and to show them the way to their fulfillment – to rediscover their divine nature.

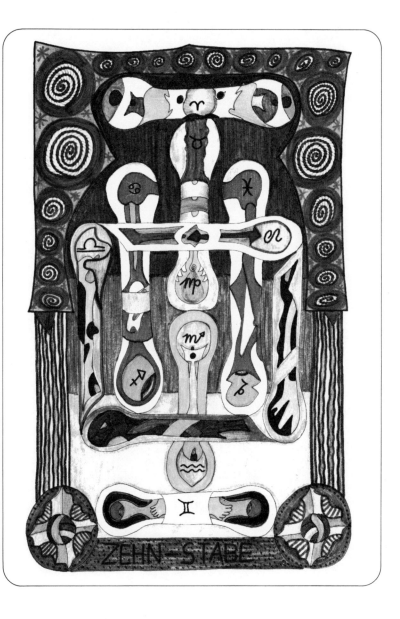

Chapter Three

THE COINS

THE SMALL, HANDY, MOBILE Coins are the next element after the massive Wands. The master of Coins is as agile as they are, understanding and manipulating his world to suit his needs.

The Wands person worked with his hands, as a farmer, a miner, or a founder of industry. Coins people saw that the farmer's produce and the miner's minerals could be bartered and sold. Coins people know things gain in worth when they are unique or available only to a privileged few. Trade is a part of a Coins mentality.

The businessmen traveled from oasis to oasis, from land to land, between China and Europe, from Africa to

America. Wherever they traded, social orders changed. The availability of luxury goods emphasized the difference between social classes, and even created class differences where none had existed. A tribal chief and his women were suddenly able to emphasize their class by dressing themselves like gods. In the Bible, the story of Solomon mentions trading with all of Africa and Asia. But when he opened the doors to trade, and the subsequent riches and fame for his people, he also opened them to the dangers of decadence, moral decay, and ruin.

The American, African and Australian aboriginal peoples are often derided for having sold gold and other indigenous treasures for just a few glass beads to the foreign traders. Yet they certainly felt they had made the better bargain – gold was so readily available to them, but who had ever seen glass before? They gained status in the eyes of their people, just as the Europeans did when they returned home with their cheaply bought gold. Nothing is of great value where it is commonly available.

The Coins represent trade with money, and also mobility of spirit or mind. Some tarot readers believe the highest revelations are hidden in the coins. Mercury, who rules the realm of trade, is also the god of swiftness, motion and agility. The Coins can be seen as the true wheels of the gypsy wagon, a symbol of the zodiac, and a representation of change and transformation.

Many events which have led to enormous upheaval were possible only because of such movement. Plants and animals were imported and exported, crossbred with native species or adapted to new environments. They became another form of the original, providing humankind with new opportunities to use them. For example, the introduction of the American potato in Europe enabled people who had only a tiny field to cultivate to raise enough food to feed an entire family.

The Coins people are as religious as any of the other castes, but they are more practical, too. Because the entire world seems to be for sale—a showplace of constant change and transformation—religion is the only constant, the only thing the trader can hold on to. The trader is a pragmatist. Religion is not a goal or a means for understanding the meaning of existence. Religion remains separate from daily life, otherwise the trader would be unable to do business comfortably with those of other faiths and customs.

Mercury, or Hermes, the god of trade and alchemy, rules the realm of Coins. This is the realm of re-evaluation and transformation.

Page of Coins

Meaning: Good news or information from the realm of Coins comes your way.

Inverted: You receive bad, incorrect, or inexact information from the realm of Coins.

Knight of Coins

Meaning: You have the support or backing of an enterprising young man from the world of money.

Inverted: Such a young man took part enthusiastically in some undertaking, but now opposes it, or alienates himself from it.

Queen of Coins

Meaning: You have good connections with a woman of Coins.

Inverted: This card inverted indicates a chain of misunderstandings with a woman of Coins, which may lead to some sort of economic danger or difficulty.

For some initiates of the modern disciplines which draw on the more or less faithfully preserved knowledge of the old Rosicrucians, the Queen of Coins is the Queen of the Earth, or she is queen over the earth-spirits—the gnomes or elves. She is an influential, powerful, and usually married woman who, either through her (or her husband's) material possessions, or her good connections, may be able to open the client's way to money needed. This card occasionally is even called a magical money magnet.

"Many beginners wishing to move through the magical world of Coins may easily overlook the influence of women in this realm," a card reader from the Camargue told us, "because they only see men seated on the visible thrones of economic power. They often forget that behind every man of Coins stands a woman, be it his secretary, wife, mistress, or mother, from whom he draws consolation or advice at the deciding moment! So if you wish to advance in this realm, remember that it is a good idea to be in good standing with the queen that is related to a powerful person.

King of Coins

Meaning: Money matters, investments, wealth, all which concerns the realm of Coins develops well.

Inverted: You will meet with opposition or unfavorable influences in matters relating to money and wealth.

The King of Coins is the King of the Earth, or he is king over the earth-spirits – gnomes and elves. He is a man with a great deal to say in financial affairs, business, matters of economy, etc. His presence always indicates a change regarding wealth, either in the form of gifts, loans, or advice having to do with money or investments.

MÜNZEN-KÖNIG

Ace of Coins

Meaning: This card represents inexhaustible economic and financial possibilities, and the best financial or economic conditions for beginning or successfully continuing a project. It also indicates economic supremacy, financial power, or the ability to deal well. (Note: In German, the word for trade, *Handel,* can also mean to bargain, do business, or to act or take action.) Occasionally, this card indicates unexpected gain, perhaps through a gamble or lottery, an inheritance, or a stock market speculation. Tarot readers who often read for people from the world of finance regard this card as the "lucky star" or the "sun of gold." These also shine benevolently on journeys—either business trips, or trips which might set a sequence of related events in motion.

Inverted: You are misjudging your economic potential!

A card reader in London once told me that no matter how large a fortune is, if you don't know the art of dealing with it, playing with it, gambling or conjuring with it, it is worth less than the possessions of a beggar. At least the beggar's meagre belongings don't hinder his travels or disturb his sleep. A large but stagnant fortune is a dangerous burden which disturbs its foolish possessor in his swim through life's seas, and can easily pull him under.

Two of Coins

Meaning: You may experience an economic or financial decline. If you do, it will be due less to your own mistakes or to opposition from others, than to the fact that, much as we try to avoid it, decline must always follow a rise in prosperity. We can use the moon as an example. Seers and occultists still remind us today that whatever increases must, occasionally, decrease. The two circles on the card illustrate this. In one we see the moon become full and radiate its inexhaustible joy and good luck onto the earth. The second reminds us of the full moon yet to come. Even if we can barely see it waning, we know the moon is in the process of disappearing. So we are masters of our fates only when we realize that each peak must inevitably give way eventually to a valley, if only to make room for another peak of good fortune.

Inverted: You experience decline and losses which will not lead to renewed prosperity. Even if your losses are slight, they may result in your subjection to another person who is financially more powerful, like a loanshark.

Three of Coins

Meaning: This card represents your acquiring the ability to emerge from an economic crisis as the victor—you can come out of it actually having gained in some way. You are learning not to crow about your successes, as well as not to lose your head about your failures. No situation or business dealing is a clear-cut either-or question.

Tarot readers who advise people in economic matters always teach that we gain something only when we pay for it on some level. Each loss is seen as a signpost indicating what doesn't work. Learn a lesson from the event and gain from it! If we think this way, always maintaining an overview instead of complaining, no matter how the wheel of fate turns, we always will remain on top of things, able to make progress at every turn.

Inverted: You experience economic or financial losses. You lost your head, just because things took an unfamiliar turn. Or, a business venture fails because you were indecisive at an important moment.

· Four of Coins

Meaning: Resistance arising from others who are developing their own economic abilities threatens to impose limits on your undertakings. This card can also indicate natural catastrophes, failed harvest or related events. No matter how extensive your own financial resources are, the titanic game in which the Coins roll around the world suddenly seems to obey an unfathomable law all its own. You cease to feel like a player, and feel like a marionette or chess piece instead. The Coin person who naively believes that money rules the world suddenly discovers that the interaction of countless, independent forces decides who succeeds and who fails.

Inverted: Your inability to see beyond the tip of your own nose—to recognize that although economics influences politics, for example, that the reverse is also true—leads to failure. You need to learn that people aren't merely consumers to be manipulated, but are living beings who, because of certain ideas, passions, a sense of honor, religious ideals, etc., are likely to act differently from what you might have expected.

VIER-MÜNZEN

Five of Coins

Meaning: You acquire a new way of correctly "playing" and increasing your wealth because you are gaining greater perspective of your world.

Inverted: You experience defeat and loss from poor investments.

Six of Coins

Meaning: Confused economic or financial influences affect your love life, passions and/or a wedding.

Inverted: You experience financial loss due to affairs of love, petty jealousies, marital tensions, or through blackmail, false expectations of inheritance, dowry or alimony.

SECHS-MÜNZEN

Seven of Coins

Meaning: Calculation and exact appraisal, as well as an objective overview of your economic possibilities, set the stage best for very big financial dealings.

Inverted: You fall prey to self-deception, sham and illusions.

Eight of Coins

Meaning: You are at a stalemate. You need to reflect upon the contradiction between your personal plans and financial possibilities on the one hand, and how these ideas relate to reality–what actually goes on in the world–on the other.

Inverted: Confusion arises because you don't understand the financial world. Because you don't understand the money game, you may feel that you can't keep up with the changing times, or you may feel old and out of it. When this card is inverted, you may need to rethink your position. For example, when things are going their way financially, people are staunch supporters of the progress society is making. But when money or career is not going so well because of poorly made personal decisions, we hear them say that times are bad. This symbolizes the "downfall of the society." Maybe you need to make some changes in your attitudes now–especially as your attitudes reflect your financial position.

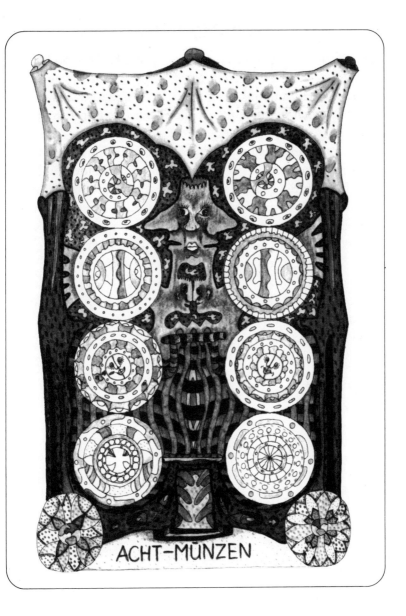

ACHT-MÜNZEN

Nine of Coins

Meaning: You are able, in an almost playful manner, to integrate all possible sources of income which you have been underestimating. Your creative imaginativeness in the realm of economics suddenly blossoms. Your supremacy in the financial realm is not merely superficial, but real and enduring, and recognized by all around you. You can use your head in financial matters and can give advice to others which is better than you might have thought possible. A Czech occultist called this the card of the alchemist who is able to transform everything he or she brews into gold. This is the card of the person who sees potential wealth even in what others call trash.

Inverted: Your lack of imagination leads to economic misfortune. Minor financial difficulties cause you to despair and fail economically.

Ten of Coins

Meaning: You are able to see the overview of any situation and have the ability to judge economic possibilities. You master the chess game of finance, and are able to see all the possible future moves and countermoves. In addition, you have a sort of sixth sense for the course of things in the realm of Coins—an intuitive feeling which is almost impossible to grasp intellectually.

Inverted: You jump to false conclusions and plan poorly in situations. You have lost your overview, and with it, your self-confidence.

Chapter Four

THE SWORDS

ACCORDING TO INDIAN LEGEND, the four "suits" or castes were created in order for each to help the others. They were also intended to impose controls on any one caste which threatened to disturb the balance by acquiring too much power. The Brahmins, the priests who preserved religious scriptures in their libraries and minds, but whose knowledge could also tend to stagnate and become empty ritual, stood next to the Kshatriyas. The word *Kshatriya* is often translated as "warrior" or "knight," which are misleading terms. These were people from well-born families. The word *gentlemen* comes closer to describing the kind of people they were. Both castes studied the scriptures, but while the priests expressed their belief in words and religious services in temples, the Kshatriyas simply expressed their belief in their daily lives.

Their tasks were to protect weaker people from oppression, to honor their ancestors, and to express the divine nature of existence by making their lives a magnificent and divine game. This highly cultivated segment of Indian society made its influence felt from Afghanistan to Indonesia, from Ceylon to Tibet. It also influenced Europe, China, Japan and Siberia.

When these two groups (or realms) fell out of balance, however, power hungry priests sought to oppress the other castes and transform the Kshatriyas into an obedient police

Figure 11. The flaming crowned Ace of Swords has always been the image of mastery over yourself and your followers. Illustration from The Primitive World, *by Court de Gebelin, Vol. 8, Paris, 1781.*

force to keep the "lower" castes in line. Long before the European Middle Ages, India was witness to terrible religious persecution under the Brahmans. If the Kshatriyas became too powerful, human rights disappeared, and only totalitarian rulers and cowering underlings remained.

The sword is not a symbol of war. It is much better understood if we think of the medieval knight on a quest, rescuing a damsel from a club-swinging giant. The club represents matter, the sword represents spirit.

The Wands and Swords both represent male energy. The Wands symbolize potency or virility as expressed in the growth of trees and plants, blazing flames, and towering mountains. Theirs is the energy that drives animals to mate in spring. The Sword is a work of craftsmanship and art. First the metal must be won from the depths of the earth, then heated with fire and cooled with water. The sword cuts swiftly through the air—like a lightning bolt. It is "the fire of the air," symbolizing the element air.

The sanguine Indian nobles followed the path of Kama, the god of love. During times of peace, they sought to make their lives a dance—a play—in which they pursued physical pleasure. The art of love was also the path to a direct experience of the divine on earth.

While the traders lived simply and filled warehouses with rich treasures from abroad, the priests lived like beggars, denouncing the accumulation of treasures as sinful while simultaneously building splendid, magnificent temples for their gods. The Kshatriyas (or nobles) simply used all that was beautiful and pleasing to decorate their homes. Even their icons were seen as objects of beauty.

The darker side of this joy in sensual pleasure was greed for possession and power. When the nobles lost sight of their bond with the divine, they lost sight of their divine task of protecting the weak, and they lost their ability to appreciate beauty.

Page of Swords

Meaning: You receive a message from the realm of swords, perhaps from the Queen of Swords. This card indicates you can expect external, tangible or internal, intangible support from other people. Your clan or family plays a large part in this. You may, for example, be accepted into an order, club, or political organization of some kind which would be an honor, promising a certain degree of social influence.

Inverted: You receive unfavorable reports from the political realm, possibly reports of war. If, for example, the person receiving a reading asks about a journey abroad, the page inverted speaks of an almost certain obstacle – a region to be traveled through will be involved in war of some kind, and it is best to re-route the journey, or cancel the entire trip.

SCHWERT-BUBE

Knight of Swords

Meaning: You receive support from a young man, or a group of young people who are very enthusiastic about beautiful old traditions (like festivals or rituals), social interaction, and love affairs.

Inverted: The card inverted represents a young man who is the opposite of political. You will be involved in a disagreement with a person whose social activity does not yet reflect hunger for power or striving for gain, but reflects high ideas.

SCHWERT-RITTER

Queen of Swords

Meaning: You are valued socially, and your company is desirable. Your appearance and presence appeal to both men and women who make you the center of attention.

Inverted: You lose the important affection of a socially influential "Queen" which makes your social progress more difficult.

Also called the Queen of Air Spirits (sylphides), this queen is the ideal of men who exercise strong influence in society. She is the wife or long-time mistress of a politician, an influential artist or a man whose life goal is to structure his life like a beautiful, well-balanced work of art. Artistically talented herself, she is the muse of artistic endeavor. She does nothing merely to do it—the path to her goal is almost more important than the goal itself. In the Indian tradition, women are divided into four basic types. The Queen of Swords represents Chitrini, the archetype of the woman of art. When preparing a meal, she will spend a great deal of time making sure the setting is beautiful, that flowers grace the table, that music plays and that the conversation is stimulating. For her, sex without romance is unthinkable. When her influence is strong, the men close to her will dress like magnificent peacocks, and their public lives will be like colorful paintings.

SCHWERT-KÖNIGIN

King of Swords

Meaning: A man like the King of Swords is your friend.

Inverted: Such a man opposes you, or some obstacles stand in your way.

Also King of the Air or Air Spirits (sylphides), this king is a strong, very masculine man who usually has dealings in the realm of politics or applied social sciences, including the science of war. He also works very creatively in the arts and is highly regarded by women who have a well-developed sense of beauty and art. The King and Queen of Swords correspond to the Emperor and Empress in the Major Arcana.

Ace of Swords

Meaning: This card represents all the abilities stemming from your family, clan or tribe, whether they are inherited, learned, or the expression of long-standing traditions. These abilities are the prerequisite for your success in society. If this card represents you in the reading, you have the potential to be a "representative of the people." You are motivated by an inner fire, life forces which allow you to spend hours on end with "your" people, holding discussions, speaking publicly, and giving everyone some of your warmth and sincerity. You know your own strengths and weaknesses, as well as those of your friends and enemies, and you also know how to best make use of them in the great chess game of life.

Inverted: You misinterpret and repress all the social knowledge and abilities you learned at home, often because of a dispute or break with your family. You make a constrained attempt to "be someone," on your own, independent of your past.

Two of Swords

Meaning: There are rifts in your relationships—misunderstandings with parents, relatives (clan or group members), friends, fellow party members, etc. But this set-back is not difficult to overcome. All that is needed is a moment's reflection over the true nature of the situation. After spending some time in contemplation, you will probably recognize that the blame is always yours. Complaining about bad parents ("They don't understand . . . "), selfish relatives, or worthless friends is silly because you always are surrounded by the people you deserve. If you were better, they would be too. We all are, in the end analysis, the products of our environments and ancestors, influenced by the thoughts and actions of the people close to us. We can't change these factors by ranting and raving or complaining, but by changing ourselves and beginning to see the world around us more clearly. Then we are well on our way to the Three of Swords.

Inverted: You may experience a set-back in the social area of your life which you refuse to understand as an invitation to self-examination. You may find yourself in a submissive situation. Someone more powerful than you may force you to propound views you don't believe in.

Three of Swords

Meaning: You find your equilibrium in society. You achieve the skill of coming out of any crisis a winner. You learn to see the actual issues rather than merely believing the slogans being bandied about.

The two ever-battling political wings which we call the right and left both present necessary but distorted images of the world. Neither of the utopian models can ever become a reality. If, in fact, one faction takes power for a while, it quickly finds itself forced to move farther and farther away from its ideals. The one-sidedness of the new regime creates unrest and dissatisfaction among more and more people until a countermovement develops and the new rulers are faced with the necessity of engaging in activities, like suppression of free speech, which may be antithetical to their ideals. Soon their reputation is destroyed, and the people dream of a swing to the opposite extreme.

The Three of Swords represents the ability to go beyond rigid political dogma to take life's middle path, and to bring viable and realizable ideals into the environment.

Inverted: You are caught in a cross-fire due to incomplete political knowledge, indecision, greed for social position, or selfishness.

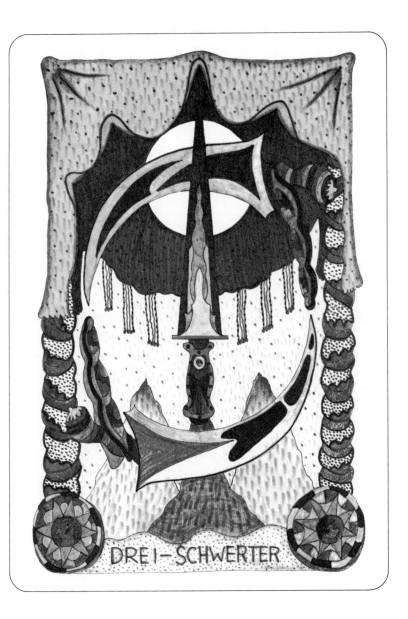

DREI–SCHWERTER

Four of Swords

Meaning: An unfamiliar lifestyle and its social rules conflict with those you know and hold to be correct. Different mores, ethics and concepts of honor dominate your environment, and you are faced with increasing resistance.

Inverted: You fail because of an inability to even superficially adjust to an unfamiliar social, political, moral or legal environment.

A gypsy from the Jena area once told me an unusual story about the gypsies of old. Before their children were full grown, they would be sent to another clan, sometimes even to settled people, to live and work. They learned to function among people of completely different life styles and customs without abandoning their own ways, and without offending or disturbing others. Russian and Polish nobles in the 19th century also sometimes sent their sons to live with friendly gypsies in order to learn to see with new eyes.

Five of Swords

Meaning: You have the ability to integrate the many elements making up your world so they will work together for you. This is the skill which, whether learned or inherited, makes a chief. With a little well-deserved help from all sides, your abilities will lead to multi-leveled success in some social or political aspect of your life.

Inverted: Disputes among family and friends hinder you in attaining your goal.

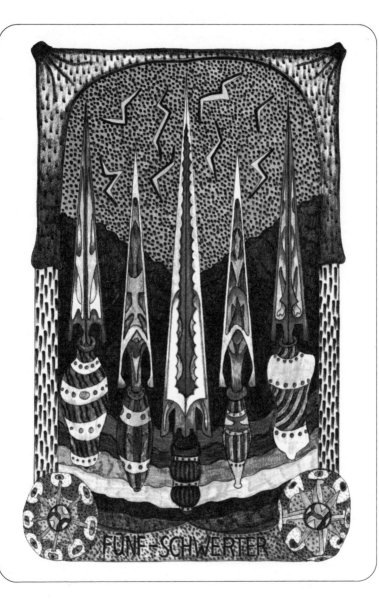

Six of Swords

Meaning: There are tensions in your marriage or love relationship because of divergent mental attitudes and opposing ideas of morality, decency, and ethics handed down by your families. It is a "quarrel of the ancestors."

Inverted: Differences in basic attitudes lead to discord with your spouse or lover. Your entire social position may be shaken, and a separation or divorce is possible.

SECHS-SCHWERTER

Seven of Swords

Meaning: You are good at dealing with a person who is close to you. You recognize this person's wishes and are able to fulfill them. You also recognize and are able to use his or her talents at the right moment to help you both approach your goal.

Inverted: Your uncertainty about your own acquired social or political position threatens to result in failure, for example, in an election.

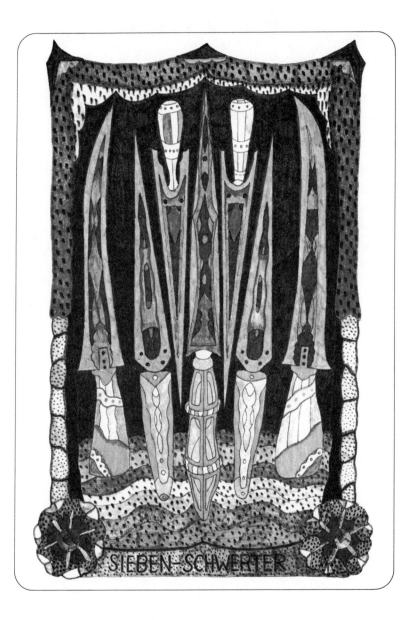

Eight of Swords

Meaning: Your political/social progress is at a standstill. The social group of which you are a member may gain in influence. You reflect on the contrasts between your own attitudes as you learned them from your family, and the attitudes of the group now in power in your life. Despite many self-congratulatory slogans, almost no country really provides equal opportunity for social and creative development to all people regardless of class, race, religion, etc. A gypsy once told me, "When we notice that the differences between ourselves and the great world around us cause more and more suffering, we sit together in a circle. We consider thoroughly how much we must adapt—or how much we can afford to—without betraying the traditions of our ancestors, or nothing else remains but to dismantle the tents once more and wander on."

Inverted: The contrast between the outer and inner world may lead you, especially if you are an artistic person, to the edge of melancholy. You may have a persecution complex or suspect a hostile conspiracy. Often, involvement in social activities or everyday tasks will help bring you out of this state.

Nine of Swords

Meaning: You finally recognize the treasure trove of possibilities which are yours, although you have underestimated them until now. These traits are available to you from your background. They may be a wealth of wisdom handed down, or skills that will help you succeed in life's struggle. They may also concern relations with others, especially with family and friends from your youth. One reader once told me this card can also indicate an inheritance which suddenly has a wonderful effect on you. For example, a book left you by your grandparents might have been considered worthless until you suddenly begin to find words of wisdom in it, as if a divine ancestor were speaking to you through its pages.

Inverted: Lack of imagination prevents you from drawing on lessons from the past (such as the mistakes of your forefathers), and leads to political and/or social misfortune. This energy may also manifest a false pride in your ancestors which arises when you do not make use of their experience, but desire to look down on other people.

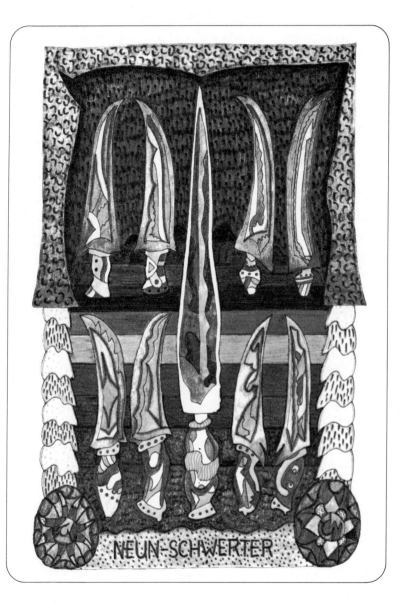

Ten of Swords

Meaning: Standing behind you are the combined energies of your entire clan, your relatives, all your acquaintances and friends. An American who learned the tarot from gypsies whose tribe lived near Mexico told me the carnival magician's table has four legs. They are the health and strength of the body, skill in dealing with coins, knowledge from the ancestors, and trust in God's goodness, angels and saints. The table can't stand on one leg, or even on three—all four are needed.

Even when the Ten of Swords has a prominent place in your reading, you can fully use the possibilities it promises only when you possess the skill of placing your entire trust in the experience of your ancestors. Gypsies say, in times of need, just let all the stories, saying and fairy tales you were told as a child run through your head. You will always find in them the example which will help you.

Inverted: You lose social influence and prestige, and important friendships.

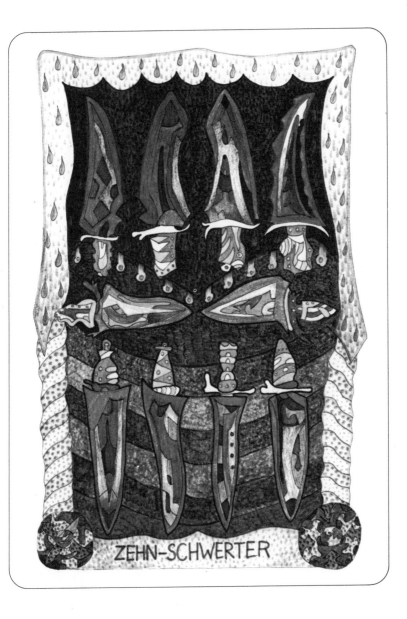

ZEHN-SCHWERTER

Chapter Five

THE CUPS

WHETHER WE THINK OF the communion cup of the Christian church, or of the vessels used by Hindu Brahmans in purification ceremonies, in nearly all known religions, a vessel, grail, or cup is the symbol for the "caste" whose occupation is to maintain the rites and rituals of religious worship.

In holy Hindu scriptures, the elixir of life, the drink of immortality called "Soma," is prepared in the moon. It spills onto the mountains as rain, is drawn into plants through their roots, and is eaten by cows. When people drink milk, the Soma rejuvenates them. It becomes sperm, capable of

Figure 12. Seven towers decorate the Ace of Cups in the old tarot. It is the image of a magical vessel filled with the miracle drink of alchemists — the drink of youth and rebirth. Illustration from The Primitive World, *by Court de Gebelin, Vol. 8, Paris, 1781.*

creating new life. It symbolizes fertility, the powers of love, and youth.

The Wands, the suit of farmers and those who work with the earth, represent the element fire. The rolling Coins, moving goods from land to land, represent the element earth. The Cups, sometimes drawn so exquisitely that they recall the Holy Grail of medieval sagas, represent the element water.

The midwife who brought my son into the world in 1961 told me she had delivered a baby for one of the gypsy folk a few days before. It was the beginning of April, still a cold time of year, yet shortly after the birth, the father took the babe to the river Emme which flows in torrents from the nearby mountains, and dipped it in. I had often heard of this practice, but always assumed it to be a folktale. An acquaintance of mine who is active in the cultural scene in the Bern area also heard accounts of this practice. He explained it to me in a way which made a great deal of sense.

The gypsies probably brought the custom with them from India, their original homeland, without changing it much. They clung to it tenaciously even though the weather conditions were much harsher in their new homeland. One gypsy told him, "I have no idea how warm the Indian rivers which were sacred to our ancestors were, but if the rivers here are much colder, the dipping takes on an even deeper significance." Survival in the European lands in harsh times may have been much more difficult than in the warmer Asian realms. If a few of the clans cling to the old custom, it is not mere thoughtless imitation of an old rite, but a lesson for the child. He should learn as soon as possi-

Figure 13. The cup depicted on older cards is reminiscent of the Holy Grail of the medieval saga. From J.G.J. Breitkopf, "Attempt to discover the origins of playing cards" (Leipzig, E. Germany, 1784), Vol. 1.

ble after birth how rugged, difficult and uncomfortable this life can be. How much warmer are the father's hands, what wonderful energy flows from them! Perhaps the first awareness dawns in the child that in all life's difficulties, the experience and friendship of family, relations, brothers and sisters are the only sure help.

What we call "cult practices" and what we regard as applied medical science constituted an indivisible unit to the ancient people. The folk of Vedic songs saw birth as a natural process as well as a religious act revealing divine forces at work. The new arrival was a reincarnation of ancestors; washing it was a matter both of hygiene and religious baptism. Birth was a celebration of an immortal soul's visit to the realm of mortals.

The Puranas, scriptures dealing with the myths of the great gods, devote entire sections to the ritual of washing.[5] Interestingly, it is said that a sign of the Kali Yuga, the age of darkness and decadence, is that people will wash themselves only in order to get clean. But the traditional laws passed down through the Brahmin caste were meant to instill spiritual purity as well as physical cleanliness. Being cleansed was like a rebirth—a renewal of life.

Maybe this is why Vishnu's first avatar, his first visible manifestation is as a fish-like creature. Theophrastus Paracelsus wrote, "Paradise was in the water, where it still is. This explains why children are still baptised nowadays."[6] When we consider the fact that the human embryo lives in fluid, and that many myths tell of the origins of all land animals (including human beings) as water creatures, we begin to see that modern science and ancient "superstition" aren't necessarily so different.

A French writer (J. Richepin) who claimed to be of gypsy descent wrote in 1888 of having heard a wise gypsy woman say these words as she dipped a child into a river, then lift it toward the sun: "Like the water you will go through everything, pass through everything, for you are free, free, free. Like the water, you will know how to sing, listen well to its song—'move, move.' Like the water you will be able to dance, just watch its dance, it tells us, 'farther, farther!' Like the water when you die, you will stream into a great ocean from which the sun again will call you back."[7]

We can see that water plays an important part in what we call religious or spiritual aspects of life. It is directly connected with the miracle of all life, so the cup, understandably, has become a religious symbol. Each caste had its own method of expressing the divine nature of existence. The Cups person is most closely associated with what we understand as religion.

Both Indian and gypsy lore tell of a golden age when the sciences reached peaks never again seen by humanity. This knowledge was used, not to serve businesspeople's greed or rulers' lust for power, but to serve the holy wise people who sought ways to better understand creation's miracle, and to bring more joy to all people. Science was a form of divine worship, praise of the wonder of creation.

Unfortunately, this view of science as religion didn't last. Momentary lack of vigilance on the part of the priest caste contributed to the decline and fall of an entire culture. When they no longer reminded their people of life's purpose and their place in creation, rulers who were power hungry took action. Those in opposition to them were killed. Priests were persecuted. Only the most degenerate of Brahmins were tolerated. Religion lost its meaning as a way of helping all beings realize the miracle of existence. It degenerated into black magic, and a means of attaining power over others. This has happened again and again throughout history. Many attempts have been made to unify science and religion, yet these attempts ended with science being dominated by religion. The Inquisition is a prime example.

So the cup represents the priesthood, which tries to shape each new or ancient truth into the form of laws and commandments to be maintained through priestly teachings and rituals.

Page of Cups

Meaning: The Page of Cups brings good news from the spiritual realm or will bring news of a meeting which promises enlightenment or progress on the path to higher realization. If you are reading the cards in regard to a purely material matter, such as a business trip, this card indicates favorable prospects. The entire affair may also take on a deeper meaning! A meeting or an acquaintance made during the trip may turn a purely financial matter into an important step on the path of understanding the meaning of life.

Inverted: This is a warning that you may easily fall prey to some influence from the spiritual realm. For example, the representative of a sect may attempt to win you over and may not hesitate to use what some call "black magic." You may also be exposed to advertising tricks, hypnosis, mind-altering drugs, etc.

Knight of Cups

Meaning: You receive friendship, stimulation and support from young people who see religion and philosophy as an important influence in their lives.

Inverted: A young man opposes you. His basic beliefs and mental attitude are the causes of the conflict.

KELCH-RITTER

Queen of Cups

Meaning: You receive support or enriching mental stimulation from a religious woman, a "lotus woman," who speaks little of her beliefs, choosing rather to realize them in her daily life. She influences both the men and women around her very strongly.

Inverted: You fail to gain such a woman as your ally.

The Queen of Cups is also called the Queen of Water and is queen over the water-spirits (undines). According to the Indian classification of the four types of women, this queen is the Padmini, or lotus woman. "Her facial features are pleasing, like the full moon, her skin is refined, tender and pale like the yellow lotus flower, her eyes are large and radiant like those of a young deer, her yoni is like an opening lotus-bud, and her love seeds (Kama salila, the water of life) is perfumed like the newly blossomed lily. She eats little, sleeps lightly and is as pious as she is clever and charming, striving always to honor the gods and delight in conversations with Brahmans."[8]

The Queen of Cups is at peace in her moral and religious convictions. Her influence allows the religions proselytized by all kinds of priests to become powerful forces in the world. Without her help, religion would remain pure ideology, castles in the air to be discussed and defended enthusiastically, but never lived.

KELCH-KÖNIGIN

King of Cups

Meaning: This card indicates you have the friendship and services of a man like the King of Cups.

Inverted: Such a man is your enemy.

The King of Cups is also called the King of Water or Water-spirits (undines). He is a "priestly" man, one who is powerful in the realm of religion, philosophy and ideology. He may emerge as a leader, but in any case, he is obviously guided in his moral behavior by his deeply held beliefs.

His friendship brings with it the blessings contained in his magic cup. They may be in the form of divine powers he bestows on those who honor him, or they may be more tangible forms of help for his followers.

The King of Cups is the keeper of some timeless wisdom, which can be received from him when he is inclined to share it. He may be a tarot reader, the teacher of some occult science, an author, a university professor, archivist, but whatever form his work takes, he is always the keeper and disseminator of spiritual treasures that are almost incomprehensible to those who come to him to learn.

Kelch-König

Ace of Cups

Meaning: The Ace of Cups symbolizes the energies drawn from the divine in the form of religion or philosophy. It represents the ability to see all your external work as an expression of your striving toward your spiritual goals. You have the feeling, even in the midst of a crisis, that you are at peace with your gods.

Interpreters of holy Indian scriptures assure us that religion is, in this sense, the business of all castes, not just of priests and monks. Our work can only be satisfying if we can see it as the expression of some greater plan. If we are convinced that our actions are meaningless within the vastness of the world, or that they are possibly harmful, and only done in order to extend our accidental existence, our vital energies quickly become depleted, and our actions produce only inferior results.

Inverted: You completely misjudge your inner or spiritual needs. For example, you may fall prey to the illusion that your needs will be met by a few hours of "recuperation" in front of the TV screen, or by sitting in a bar now and again discussing existential questions like, "What does modern science say about the immortality of the soul?" or "How can we compare Buddha, Jesus and Marx?"

Two of Cups

Meaning: Difficulties reconciling your personal vision of the world with reality plague you. Belief systems you grew up with and never questioned no longer seem absolute and you feel confused. You can use this situation as an opportunity to consciously review the beliefs you have held until now. If you do so thoroughly and honestly, you will move on to a new stage in your development.

Inverted: Your image of the world is crippling you. The things you thought you believed in seem to desert you, and the consolation they gave you is lost, as if the contents of a cup had leaked away into a dry, infertile desert. You cling to the mere trappings of beliefs whose spirit is dead; faith is reduced to superstition and gods are replaced by ghosts. You carry out empty rituals, like going to church on Sunday, joylessly, because you have nothing better. You embrace an ideology out of fear—who knows what comes after death?—more than from the hope or conviction that it will sustain you and inspire you to carry on.

ZWEI·KELCHE

Three of Cups

Meaning: You discover your inner balance! You now have the ability to maintain your equilibrium in a crisis. There is no conflict any more between religious beliefs learned in childhood, modern scientific theory, the so-called atheism of many Westerners, and the unfathomable joy in Indian mysticism, because you have gained a higher perspective on things. This lends you an inner equilibrium which makes you appear "priestly" in a positive sense. You provide peace and balance to the people in your circle and are able to show them how to step out of their chaos. You can help alleviate, to some extent, their doubt in God and the world (and by extension, in themselves). The Three of Cups represents the beginning of a very important realization. The sphinx questions ("Who am I?" "Where do I come from?" "Where am I going?") are pushing you to develop a philosophy that influences your life.

Inverted: You miss the opportunity to transform a defeat into an inner victory because you are not growing at this time.

DREI-KELCHE

Four of Cups

Meaning: You are confused by the variety in this world. In your bewilderment, you lose or are unable to find a clear goal in life. The truths contained in holy books, whether they are the four Vedas or the four gospels, seem to stand in direct opposition to each other. If the Four of Cups represents you, you feel like a leaf blown from all directions. You are at wit's end, and come to a standstill on all levels. Only by clearly thinking over your situation will you progress to the Five of Cups, the pentagram.

Inverted: You are wasting your energies in a constant chase from one fashionable religion, sect or ideology to another. This unsettledness may lead rapidly to a breakdown on all levels, including family life, career, economic matters, and/or health.

Five of Cups

Meaning: You approach the "star of hope and mercy," with the conviction that all your actions have a deeper meaning. You see things with new eyes and experience what some call a "mystical rebirth," which influences all your thoughts and actions.

Inverted: You exchange your potential view of the world for one which is immeasurably worse (more negative). This is the modern equivalent of selling one's soul to the Devil.

FUNF-KELCHE.

Six of Cups

Meaning: This card represents doubt regarding love and goodness. It indicates the loss of the ability to see—behind all the forces at work in the world—a greater plan helping all beings toward their development. This condition can lead to a much more dangerous internal crisis than if you were just vacillating between the truths of two different religions.

Inverted: You think that hate, evil, or the struggle for survival really rules the world. This leads to an inability to evolve positive, constructive, or mutually beneficial relationships. According to one experienced card reader, this feeling can also lead to escape into alcohol or hard drugs.

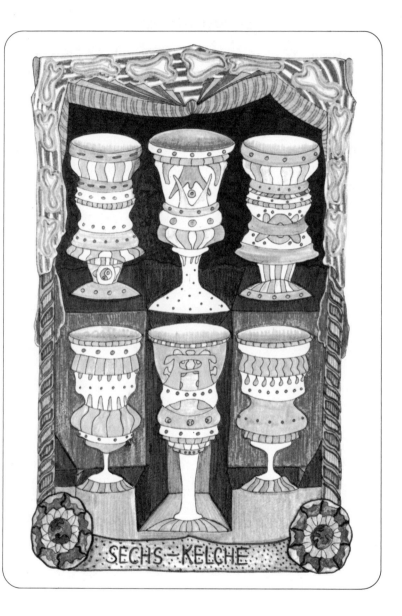

Seven of Cups

Meaning: You are initiated into a body of ideas which completely corresponds to your inner needs. This results in the development of all your creative talents.

Inverted: You're stuck in an ideological dead end. You mishandle a situation because of your one-sided ideology, attitude, or philosophy. You violate your own happiness, and that of others close to you.

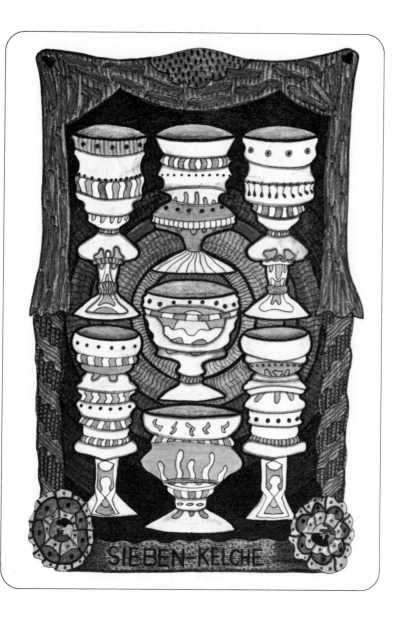

Eight of Cups

Meaning: Your concept of the material world and your religious ideals don't mesh, which can lead you to withdraw or retreat inwards. The divine seems impossible to realize here, so the "beyond," in the form of paradise or heaven in another dimension or even another planet, becomes your focus. In any case, this card represents difficulty in attaining a goal because you regard it as unattainable. You think that such a thing would be too beautiful for this earthly vale of tears.

The positive aspect of this card is that you possess great powers of imagination and fantasy, and the ability to create a rich inner world for yourself. In addition to achieving something external and visible for yourself, you have a means of realizing something through the use of your imagination which will benefit humanity.

Inverted: You tend to escape, perhaps into a religious belief which excuses your every failure in that it views human happiness as not present here, or teaches that it is only attainable in the beyond.

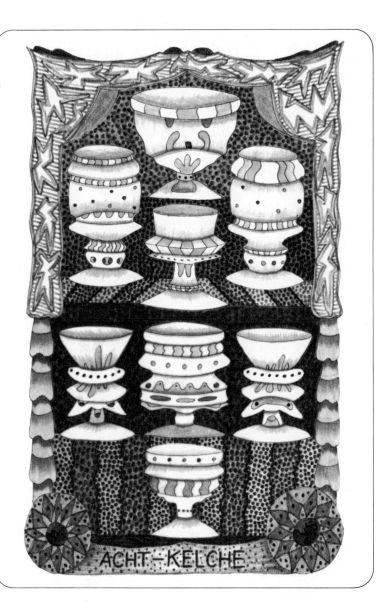

Nine of Cups

Meaning: You recognize that in this world, we can only judge the rightness of religions and ideologies according to their fruits. The Nine of Cups represents finding a way to bring the daily tasks of life, such as marriage, childrearing, and career more into harmony with your inner ideals.

Inverted: You've lost faith. Your entire idealism is shattered by a task which appears impossible to do, impossible to carry out according to your ideals. There is danger that your world, as you have worked to establish it so carefully over a long period of time, could fall apart. This could include a marriage or close relationship.

Ten of Cups

Meaning: You are calmly aware of the divine meaning in the way of the universe, which may appear bewildering to others.

Inverted: You suffer from inner chaos.

Chapter Six

THE MAJOR ARCANA

COURT DE GÉBELIN, THE first person to research the origins of the tarot cards, was a scholar and leading thinker of the Freemasons in the 18th century. He called the gypsies the people actually responsible for spreading the tarot through Europe. Unfortunately, documentation about the occult sciences at that time is scarce—too much knowledge all too easily led to the burning stake. Later researchers almost always concurred that, somehow, the gypsies and the cards belonged together. Eliphas Lévi, who tried to reestablish the entire science of magic based on the tarot, thought the gypsies were incapable of devising symbolic images of such great worth, but did confirm that the gypsies had been the *keepers* of the knowledge over the centuries.[9]

Since this is still true 200 years later, we can assume it was always so. European nomads still claim to possess "a secret book, older than all others known to humanity, the one true guide to divination with cards."[10]

An Indian card game may well share common roots with the tarot. It draws heavily on ancient religious symbolism. The game has ten divisions of ten cards each. Each division represents one avatar, or incarnation of Vishnu. Each avatar appeared on earth to help all beings develop. The cards of each division are decorated with symbols representing the major deeds of the avatar in that incarnation.[11] The *Bhagavad Purana* mentions 22 avatars of Vishnu.[12] Obviously, a game with 22 sets of 22 cards would have become too unwieldy. A logical solution would have been a game with four divisions to represent Vishnu's four arms, which also represent the four elements, the four castes, etc. Even in 18th century Europe, the four suits were associated with four social classes (farmer, trader, warrior/noble, and priest), and the four elements.

Eliphas Lévi, who actually opposed the proponents of Indian philosophy, may also have conjectured the tarot's origins in India. In his manuscripts about the history of the cards, drawings of the avatars of Vishnu were found with the notation "tarot Indien," or, "tarot images from India."[13]

Court de Gébelin read the 22 Major Arcana from back to front, and saw in them a history of the world. He interpreted them as depicting the downfall of humanity from the Golden Age, a time when humanity was close to God, to a time when priests and worldly rulers dominate the masses.[14] Gypsy magicians often prefer to see the cards as a representation of their tribes' migration to the West.[15] Perhaps the card The Magician symbolizes re-discovery of the wisdom lost on the way—wisdom which would lead us back to our true source, our goal in this life.

Court de Gébelin tried, using medieval chronicles, to prove that people saw the tarot as remnants of a despicable heathenism, satanical entertainment, black magic, or damnable sorcery, as soon as the images arrived in Europe. They attempted to wipe out their use within the realm of Christianity by forbidding their use and persecuting their users. Later writers didn't refute these claims. Even today, some people still call the tarot "The Devil's Bible," saying the cards were made by the Devil and spread throughout the world by his faithful followers. So now let's look at the Major Arcana of the gypsies.

0 or 22 The Fool

Meaning: You feel the impulse toward self-contemplation, the beginning of the path to yourself.

Inverted: You make mistakes which you once again fail to learn from.

This card represents the human being, or our consciousness, at the beginning of the adventure, the endless search after experience and realization. It is also symbolic of the condition of being in hell—the path to which is paved with good intentions, as the saying tells us. The pilgrim directs his gaze toward all the wonderful goals and fails to pay attention to his immediate surroundings. Any dog can bite him, rip his trousers, hurt him with impunity. The magic flower of joy growing in his path goes unnoticed—he'll probably trample it in his heedless stumbling. This is the same flower which grows in front of the Magician's table, representing fully utilized potential.

Paracelsus, and other great authorities on the occult sciences of the wandering folk, tirelessly assured in their writings that we don't need rare, expensive curatives from far-off exotic lands. If we search carefully around our own huts, we will always find exactly the wonder-herb we need. We can assume that these magicians of old intended this advice to apply to all of life's situations, not just to physical healing. They taught, as did the Indian tantrics, "What is here is everywhere, what is here is nowhere."

Whoever seeks paradise, wisdom, joy, or the divine far away, in the past or future, loses his one and only true possession—the fulfilled moment, the present.

21 The World

Meaning: This symbolizes the successful conclusion of a matter, the new creation of your own world, the beginning of a new game, or an attempt to reorganize your possibilities from a new vantage point. Curiosity and sensual joy in existence arise, as do new temptations and seductions.

Inverted: You suffer from boredom and surfeit.

Four symbols—a winged person, an eagle, a bull and a lion—surround a magic circle, a floral wreath, or the "cosmic egg." These are the four basic forces which create the visible world and simultaneously allow us to interpret it. They also stand for the four holy scriptures (the Christian scriptures or the ancient Indian Vedas) as well as the four heads of Brahma, the god of creation, the four elements, the four heavenly directions, etc.

In the center, the world—a female figure—dances her dance of life. She is the Anima Mundi of the alchemists, the Maya of Indian philosophy and religion. This is the beginning of creation, the dream of a complete world full of enjoyment brought into being by the endless magical forces of the divine.

In some tarot decks, the dancing woman holds a wand with a globe at either end in each hand. This globe represents the four basic elements which create and comprise the bewildering abundance of this world. In Walter Wegmüller's tarot, these have become two flowers—an expression of fun—joy in the game of life.

20 The Judgement

Meaning: You experience resurrection from the grave of your own lethargy. You feel joy in "nakedness," the recognition that many very superficial things we deem necessary for our comfort just hinder our progress. You gain new lust for life through a new life-companion or child (perhaps from an earlier life).

Inverted: You are confused. What you thought was a new beginning was just an illusion—and it failed anyway. This might be the result of mistakenly placing your faith in some sect or political party, for example.

In most decks, this card represents the Last Judgement, the day when God will cause the dead to rise from their graves to be judged for their sins. Court de Gébelin calls this card "the Creation," seeing in it the creation of man and woman from earth, exactly as described by the ancient religions.[16]

According to Indian philosophy, every genesis is preceded by countless destructions and rebirths that have occurred over the aeons, so that the ages form a cycle or continuum. Thus, the different names for this card are not contradictory.

On this card, we see the sun's golden disc in the background (as on the Star, number 17) lending its light as the people rise from their dark graves to find each other and begin life's game again.

19 The Sun

Meaning: Your situation improves rapidly as a result of your more loving interaction with the people and creatures in your immediate environment.

Inverted: You lose the assistance of friends and relatives because at an earlier time you selfishly denied them what they needed or wanted from you.

The Sun pours its radiance as droplets of blessing down on two children. In some decks, the children are enclosed in a fairy's circlet,[17] which may be a low wall enclosing a garden of paradise, or a fence overgrown with lush sunflowers. On this card in the Tarocchi dei Visconti, two child angels hold a circle or sphere on which we see depicted a palace on an island surrounded by the rolling seas and a starry sky.[18] This medieval representation makes clear that the card 19 (the Sun) is to be seen as a continuation of 21 (the World), and 20 (the Last Judgement).

The pair, symbolizing a society of "new" people, receives the heavenly world of the Sun as a divine gift on earth, and it becomes their immediate reality—an earthly paradise.

Whether the children (one male, one female) dance or embrace lovingly, the meaning of the card is clear—a whole and holy world, protected from harm by divine powers. Its inhabitants are as blissful as Adam and Eve in the garden after the creation.

Christian and Indian mystics saw this condition not as having been hopelessly lost through original sin, but accessible to those who found their ways back to pure compassion.

18 The Moon

Meaning: You find a good solution because you remember the advice and guidance of parents and ancestors, and you respond to your intuition.

Inverted: Your efforts lead to failure because you don't dare to listen to your intuitive self.

A path leads past two dogs guarding mysterious ancient buildings or watchtowers. The path leads through the darkness to the depth of the waters.

The crab is a creature which always arouses amazement because of its strange sidewards motion. The constellation of Cancer in the sky leads us after the solstice into winter's darkness.

The Moon represents turning around, or diving into the depths of our all too often repressed darker sides – to the subconscious and the ancestral traditions which slumber there.

The superstitious of all ages have seen this path as terrible. The night is seen as a symbol of evil, and the gypsies who move through it have always been accused of "moon worship," or were considered to be black magicians in league with the devil. People used to claim to have seen ghosts and vampires dancing with Satan among old ruins, and dogs slinking around at dusk seemed to be bloodthirsty werewolves or vampires. We find oral and written accounts from nearly all European lands proving that the clans of the wandering gypsy folk were the ones who sought refuge in broken-down houses, abandoned alpine huts or ruins, and whose four-legged companions set the fearful residents trembling in terror of goblins, fairies and spirits.

17 The Star

Meaning: The Star indicates a situation which improves in every aspect, justifying all your hopes for a good future.

Inverted: The chance for a new beginning is lost because of your insecurity and fear of letting go of old habits.

Also called the dawn, rebirth, Venus, spring, the Star woman, flower girl, etc., the Star is glorified in the ancient Vedic songs as Ushas, goddess of Dawn. She is a fantastically beautiful woman whose appearance aroused the poets to express themselves in passionately sensuous words.

For the people of that era, each morning was a joyous event, like the meeting of lovers. Each morning was a new beginning after the dark night – a re-creation of the world.

In the Visconti tarot of the 15th century, we see a woman holding a star in her hand. Her sky-blue dress is decorated with countless golden symbols, each of which radiates downward toward the earth. She stands on a patch of green grass at the edge of an abyss. Is she the fairy who brings abundant joy from the high mountain of the gods to the people in the valleys below?

In the tarot deck acknowledged by Court de Gébelin in the 18th century as being very old, the Star shows a flower with a butterfly, a clear representation of rebirth and the resurrection – the new spring of life, of morning, of the victory of blossoming over death, night, and winter. In Wegmüller's tarot, the figure is surrounded by butterflies and star flowers, with the power of the sun behind her, the only one in the deck attempting to step out of her picture.

Die Sterne

16 Destruction (The Tower)

Meaning: External, political, social, or economic change and upheaval bring an opportunity for your advancement or ascent in some way.

Inverted: This indicates damages you have suffered due to your participation in projects that are hollow and destructive. Before getting involved, you failed to fully consider their meanings and aims.

Indian mythology is full of stories about the Asuras, which are usually called demons or titans. The word Asura really means non-suras, or non-gods. Sura is a divine intoxicating drink. The gods, or devas, are beings who see themselves, and the world, as an expression of the divine, and are continually intoxicated by this wonderful vital perception. The Asuras, ever sober,[19] attempt to make do without the divine. They masquerade as all-powerful rulers, let themselves be worshipped as earthly gods, and try to rule the heavens using their skill in building and producing mysterious machines.

"In Indian histories, attempts to implement an up-to-date social order are described again and again. A demonic ruler tries to set up an order according to the 'tamas guna.' He conquers the entire world . . . and everyone must pay homage to him as the one god. No one hungers in his realm, yet all beings groan under the crippling weight of his rule . . . he rules the world, but has no peace. While he indulges in pleasure, the so-called 'six inner enemies' plunder his heart; they are rage, lust, greed, pride, jealousy and blindness."[20] According to Indian scriptures, the megalomaniacal plans of the asuric rulers failed repeatedly because of the inner poverty of their conceivers—even the names of their grand cities are now forgotten.

15 The Devil

Meaning: Your basic energies are increasing, and, if you implement them correctly, they will supply you with all you need to experience success.

Inverted: You feel overcome by myriad desires arising from subconscious physical urges. You are unable to see a way to utilize and satisfy them rationally.

Also called the Horned One, the Black Magician, the Witches' god, the Devil was seen by the superstitious as the epitome of evil. His presence in the tarot deck was taken as proof that the tarot was an expression of dark and evil magic and Satanism. Leland, one of the greatest gypsy researchers, makes an important point, however. In the advanced culture of ancient India from which the gypsies come, there is no Satan.

The Indian god Shiva, the Destroyer, is dressed in a tiger's pelt and holds a trident (devil's pitchfork?) in his hand. On his head glows a crescent moon, which can easily be mistaken for a pair of horns. The wild night-time festivals of the Shiva-Tantric devotees were similar to those of European witches' sabbaths.

Does this ecstatic, intoxicated, sensual dance in the round form the basis of all similar cults in the world? Pan, fauns, Dionysian demon-dancers, Slavic wood-gnomes, the masked "wild folk" of the Alpen shepherds could all be related. All witches' groups in Europe see the "Horned One" as a symbol of the life forces of the universe as expressed through growth, virility, fertility, and health.

14 Temperance

Meaning: You have good fortune because you acquire the ability to put yourself in your opponent's shoes to learn something for yourself.

Inverted: You have an accident or loss because of your own stubbornness, blindness, or one-sided perspective.

Temperance does not mean the absolute abstinence from the satisfaction of certain human urges, such as sex or the enjoyment of meat, although certain "religious" or "natural science" sects would have you believe so.

Temperance means exactly what it says—to temper or moderate your behavior. (In German, the word is "Mässigkeit" from "Mass" meaning "measure," i.e., knowing the proper measure.) This does not mean abstinence, but understanding that everything in the universe has its counterbalance. As Paracelsus, the great physician who worked from an alchemical and magical perspective, taught, there are no poisons and no curatives per se. Any substance can be either, depending on the measure or dosage.

On our card, the female figure pours tirelessly from one container into the other so that both remain full. She has wings and wears a star on her head, showing herself to be an Apsara—the Indian word for fairy or swan-maiden. She is like an angel or goddess. Perhaps the containers represent the sun and moon, male and female, spirit and matter, day and night. Everything is charged with power by its opposite pole, so one-sidedness leads to destruction, unless we can perform the magical act of finding the proper antidote from time to time on the side which appears to be opposite us.

Die Mässigkeit

13 Death

Meaning: You need to let go of whatever is dead, stagnant, or frozen in your life – something that you do just from force of habit, without any enthusiasm. New possibilities, perhaps a rebirth, will result.

Inverted: You're disappointed with your life as it now is. You may tend to see life as meaningless turmoil because of failed plans. You tend to indulge in fruitless worrying.

In Indian lore, Shiva dances in graveyards and cremation grounds. His ghostly hordes make music with human bones, rub themselves with ashes, and play with skulls. But behind the horror of this gruesome dance, the peaceful and beautiful face of the eternal god is visible, giving devotees the certainty that all destruction is only illusory. After the bodies or the manifestations of a culture have decayed, a renaissance or rebirth comes – a constantly self-renewing victory of life.

So Death swings his sickle on the tarot card, but actually only in order to clear room for the new. Beneath his dancing feet, two crowned heads grow like flowers. They are those who are conscious enough to recognize that death represents merely a door to new delights and experiences.

12 The Hanged Man (The Test)

Meaning: If you now try to find meaning in your present difficulties, you will learn a lesson which will lead to success in your external and internal life.

Inverted: You are addicted to childish self-deception, bewildering dreams, empty hoping. You cannot correctly assess your situation and draw conclusions or learn lessons from it.

This symbol doesn't appear in the medieval church, but recalls the Indian yogis who gain control over body and soul by doing strenuous exercises. It also reminds us of the experience of Odin, the Germanic god, in the Edda; he hung nine icy nights from a windblown tree, in order to gain the wisdom of the runes.

Douglas called this card, "one of the clearest hints that the tarot trumps originally were designed to illustrate certain non-Christian religious beliefs."[21]

Walter Wegmüller's tarot shows the tested man hanging, not from the traditional beam and rope, but from a violin and bow. This image is based on an experience he and I shared in the fifties, in the Seefeld Alps, above the village of Habkern. At a boisterous party, a man who was a descendant of the gypsies performed an amazing feat by wrapping his legs around one of the massive beams in the ceiling and, while hanging upside-down, playing his dance melodies on the violin. He later told us that in the olden days a minstrel had to be able to do the same thing, in order to show that no position is too uncomfortable for him to give other people joy.

11 Strength

Meaning: Even if the situation seems totally confusing, you must have the courage to act. If you can master yourself—find peace in your own mind—peace, calm and love will surround you.

Inverted: You fail because you aren't realizing your own inner source of power. You don't see your true potential.

This is force, energy, the conqueror, the spirit which masters matter. We sometimes see a male sun-hero vanquishing a lion on this card, like Hercules or Samson did. But usually it is a calm and beautiful woman who appears to fearlessly hold the King of Beasts in her hand without the least effort. Her hat reminds us of the Magician's hat, and the brim also shapes an eight on its side—the symbol for eternity.

Shiva, the Indian god so important to the tantric tradition, steps on the back of a lion to mount his steed, the bull Nandi, who was said to be as white as the mountain of all joy. In ancient fables and myths, the lions are the kings of all beasts, the perfect representation of the beastly, or animal, qualities in human (and all other) beings.

"Greed leads inevitably to dissipation. If your eating habits are chaotic, you will never have any self-control."[22]

Die Kraft

10 The Wheel of Fortune

Meaning: Your situation is undergoing a welcome change.

Inverted: Your situation is changing, but you don't see the meaning behind the change, so you experience it as misfortune.

This is also the wheel of fate or karma. Two dog-like creatures are whirled endlessly in circles. If they could calmly consider for a moment what is going on, it would seem meaningless to them.

Our desires motivate us to act, to seek the way to attain the peak of fulfillment. Once we arrive on top, we are disappointed to see our goals were just illusions. It is said that people sacrifice the joys of youth in order to get on in life and provide something better for their children. When they are older, they are amazed and hurt to discover that their children despise them and call them bourgeois. Their children dream only of a free life. The farmer's son leaves the country for the city to improve his standard of living, but once his goal is achieved, his only desire is to spend his last years in an isolated little cottage in the country.

This card shows us the only way out of our never-ending cycle of illusions. We must find the sphinx-like inner peace within ourselves. We need to recognize that life's purpose is not to make a big splash, but to take delight in and enjoy the things that the so-called seekers of bliss generally miss—blooming flowers, the game of love, dancing children, total physical health, or the beauty in every moment.

Das Glücksrad

9 The Hermit

Meaning: You should take the advice of a hermit, a guru, or someone who has rediscovered ancient wisdom. Sometimes as we struggle along through times of great tension, we don't take the time to consider such advice because it seems a waste of time. If you listen and follow the advice you are given, it will suddenly show you a path you are overlooking because of your restlessness.

Inverted: You refuse help out of a false sense of pride and an inflated estimation of your own abilities. You close your ears to the voice of experience. You are unable to calmly consider your questions and discuss them with others wiser than yourself.

The Hermit, carrying the light of realization, seeks his truth both by night and by day. Gypsy occultists sometimes see in him the Old Man of the Mountains, the head of a medieval Oriental sect said to have passed down his teachings to the Indian nomads during their wanderings toward the West.

Some researchers suggest that the crusaders and other medieval travelers to the Orient were "infected" by the ancient heresies of Asia, and brought them back to the West. In fact, they may have brought the first tarot cards to Europe, according to these scientists.

A gypsy woman from Bern told me, "A sage who says he is wise is a fool. A sage who says he is a fool is wise."

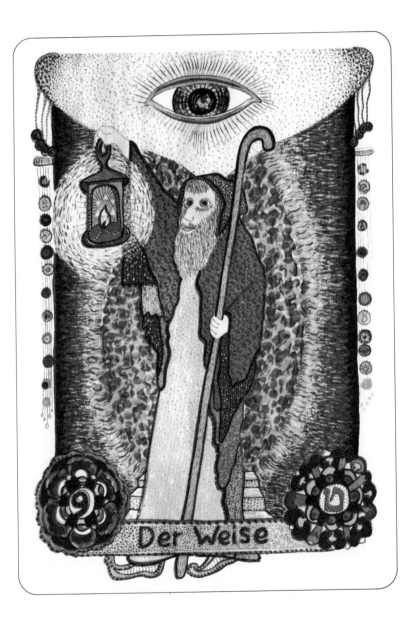

8 Justice

Meaning: You now have a good opportunity to establish a better balance between the outer and inner self–body and soul.

Inverted: Your equilibrium is disrupted, and this can have a detrimental effect in all areas of your life–ranging from legal proceedings, to problems with neighbors or other people close to you. You may also experience some kind of illness that occurs because you have neglected either your internal or your external work.

Justice also means equilibrium. When we lose our balance, we suffer–sometimes under the judge's sword. If our lives are spent in spiritual search, we may be disappointed if we are unable to utilize some of our realizations on the material plane–to spread a little joy around. On the other hand, a life spent only in a struggle for material gain is ugly. No success, no matter how enviable it may be, consoles us when we realize we have used up our life energies in achieving it; those energies are diminished, and death slowly approaches. Money, titles, awards, and any other material possessions are powerless to comfort us in the face of that reality.

Only those whose two cups are equally full can stand up to the judgment of their personal court. External activities provide experience to further our internal development, which, in turn, gives us the energy to continue satisfying activity.

7 The Chariot

Meaning: You approach your own middle path, which, when you follow it, will lead you to unimaginable success.

Inverted: A one-sided attitude is creating conflict within yourself, as well as between you and your friends. This rapidly leads to increasing failure.

The chariot driver is the victor, the triumphant one. With superior mastery, he reins in his two steeds – two somewhat unusual creatures that symbolize two opposing forces. The charioteer uses his powers correctly because he has faith in himself, so he is always master of the moment. He sits calmly, not letting himself be diverted to the right or left.

This image is reminiscent of a popular Indian icon which seems almost to be a combination of cards 7 and 6. A divine driver stands calmly and proudly in his chariot. Three lions attempt to draw it to the left and three others attempt to draw it to the right. Despite their efforts – or perhaps because of them – he is able to keep to the middle path, with the help of the seventh lion. Above him, as a symbol of his whole and holy world, are three figures. Vishnu/Krishna, the preserver of all life, stands between his wives, "the two Lakshmis" who represent inner and outer bliss, the fulfillment of inward searching and external striving. The two may seem to be mutually exclusive, but they are actually mutually dependent and, in fact, only possible when done together.

6 The Lovers (The Decision)

Meaning: You are in a very fortunate position! Two door-ways to the development of your potential stand open to you.

Inverted: You have hastily chosen what appeared to be the easier path, which may lead you to waste what is best in you by not making use of it.

This card is usually called the Lovers. However, Indian philosophy teaches that whenever we make a decision we have four possibilities open to us rather than just the two we usually are aware of. We can choose one of the two obvious possibilities, or we can choose not to choose, or we can choose both and try to integrate two apparently opposite paths.

Court de Gébelin saw in this card a young man and woman being brought together by a priest (or, perhaps, since the tarot is rooted in non-Christian cultures, by a priestess?). In this deck we see a man standing between two women. The women seem to be behaving in a contradictory way. Each seems to be drawing him nearer with one hand while fending him off with the other.

The man's clothing is colorful, and reveals that he partly favors one, partly the other. First he will be appealing to one of the women, then to the other. If he decides to stay with only one or the other, he may feel fulfilled, but will have to sacrifice half of his being.

5 The Hierophant

Meaning: Support and assistance come to you from some truth that has either been handed down from your ancestors, or that you read about or heard from another person. You now are certain that you are on the "right" path.

Inverted: You've reached a dead end. Your belief system is full of empty slogans that have long ago lost their once holy meanings.

Also called the Pope, the Magus of the Eternal, the Brahman, the Master of the Church, the Hierophant is one of the highest representatives (archetypes) of the spiritual realm. He leads souls to their highest goal, using the path of traditions, rites and formulas that have been handed down from the past. He is surrounded by symbols, and, depending on which deck you use, you may recognize them as deriving from Indian, Egyptian, Jewish or medieval Christian tradition.

One tarot reader told me that it doesn't matter which church we think of when we see this card. He is simply the bishop or head of any established religious community which sees itself as the only bearer of the truth. He also sees other people as heretics and pagans.

In the Wegmüller tarot, the Hierophant's head is full of countless books from all the ages. He knows all of them by heart. He sits on a throne of rock, symbolizing his solid, unshakable truth. Devotees of the direct experience of divinity – in the form of catharsis, shamanism or ecstatic tantra – have always seen this truth as petrified. For them, it is a tombstone of inner development.

4 The Emperor

Meaning: You will meet someone who will be a strong positive example to you, or a positive authority figure. This person will help you gain the self-control you need to advance on your path. You can also see that power and will are best expressed by thinking out your moves as though you were playing an intense chess game. Ranting and raving does not express power, but rather indicates you have many inner fears.

Inverted: Your plans are unsuccessful.

The Emperor is also called the War Lord, the Powerful One, the Morning Sun, etc. The eagle and the peculiar crown have led some people to claim that this image arose when some of the most important gypsy bands were still in Eastern Europe under the rule of the Russian counts, before the German Roman emperor ruled, because his crown was different.

The cube-like throne can be a symbol for the laws of the material world. The Emperor's power derives from his exact knowledge of these laws. The sphere in his hand shows his ability to integrate the chaos of the earthly desires and forces surging around him. His self-discipline allows him to make sense of and utilize them. The magic wand, the scepter in his other hand, symbolizes his awareness and mastery of his male powers, which give him an air of complete security.

3 The Empress

Meaning: Luck, progress, and a wealth of ideas that enrich your daily life are indicated. Your thoughts soar because love fills you with enthusiasm. You become open to the beauty of the arts.

Inverted: You are subject to losses resulting from fruitless passions, illusion, pretense, fata morgana.

In Indian mythology, the priest caste (Brahman) and the nobles (Kshatriya) fought each other with the assistance of their gods and magicians for world domination. The basic differences in their philosophies are reflected in, among other things, their images of the ideal woman.

One was the virtuous, moral, humble woman who fully supported her Brahman husband in his divine service to the gods. The other was the lady-in-waiting who had mastered the "64 arts," above all the art of love, and was knowledgeable in the art of magic. She was probably the heroine of those tantric gatherings in which the man and woman became one with the gods at the moment of ecstasy.[23]

This latter practice was part of the path to enlightenment which utilized sensory and extra-sensory mystical experiences rather than strict adherence to precepts and customs.

Although the High Priestess and the High Priest (Hierophant) are separated by two cards, the winged Empress with her starry crown is directly next to the Emperor. She is his companion, his ideal, the object of his desires who continually motivates him and gives him courage.

2 The High Priestess

Meaning: Things will take a turn for the better if you take the advice of a woman. Once you start following certain natural laws which you have neglected until now, you will feel re-energized.

Inverted: You are confused because you fear the feminine aspect. Your health may be ruined if you continue to ignore your physical conditions and needs.

While the Emperor and Empress play together and complement each other, the High Priest and High Priestess oppose each other. They represent patriarchy and matriarchy which, throughout human history, have often stood in opposition, and struggled for supremacy.

If the High Priest is the governor of mind who puts everything in order and attempts to subject all to his rule, the Priestess is the wise woman, the sorceress. She serves the "Great Mother," the moon, and she reads from the Book of Nature. She is seer of the ebb and flow of life. The Priest teaches liberation from matter, the Priestess teaches discovery of the eternal powers in our environment. In ancient cultures as well as in modern occult religions, she heals the body, knows fertility potions, and is an herbalist and midwife.

The last two cards represent the wise woman and the fair-ground magician, both so important in the gypsy tradition. Some people see them as further proof that the tarot originated with the nomads from India.

1 The Magician

Meaning: You will be victorious in your major endeavor because of your ability to effortlessly translate unconventional ideas into action.

Inverted: You gamble away your opportunities because of shyness. You tend toward despondency, and lack faith in your creative ideas.

In the tarot of Marseilles, the Magician stands alone on a mountain. He is a master, and no longer has any opponents in the world. He no longer needs an audience because he doesn't act out of a sense of inadequacy or a need to prove himself. His actions are a joyous game.

In the Wegmüller tarot, as in some others, the brim of the Magician's hat, as well as the table, form the symbol for eternity – an 8 on its side. It is also the symbol of duality abolished, of the recognition of the divine nature of both friends and foes. The two halves of the 8 can be seen as two magic mirrors endlessly reflecting the same image back and forth.

The blossoming flower, the peacock feathers in his hat, and the symbols for the four castes or elements on the table, all indicate his knowledge of the abundant beauty in the world, and the countless opportunities for utilizing these objects. Of course, he will use them out of sheer joy in creation's magnificence, and the game of life. He no longer has any desire to accumulate wealth or power. We can easily understand why many modern tarot readers see this card as the epitome of the loftiest magic, or even of God, who created the world and all its beings for his own amusement.

Part Three

HOW TO READ
THE CARDS

Chapter Seven

BUYING AND CARING FOR YOUR CARDS

ONE IMPORTANT RULE concerning the acquisition of your tarot cards (as well as any books or articles of magic) is, never try to bargain or drive the price down—never even imagine doing so! This is an old rule, mentioned repeatedly in folktales handed down over the centuries. Of course, people have always attributed this rule to gypsy cunning—they prevented their superstitious customers from daring to refuse to pay the often exorbitant cost of the articles they desired. But this rule expresses deep insight into the human soul. An herbalist from Bern explained its wisdom to me this way: We are generally incapable of holding a conviction and its opposite at the same time. If we try, we become increasingly absorbed in contradictions until our inner debate prevents us from acting at all. So when we put all our skill and effort into driving the price of an object lower by implying (or openly claiming) it to be less than perfect, or doubting its authenticity or effectiveness and otherwise finding fault with it, we are not likely to value it wholeheartedly once we obtain it. While convincing the dealer to lower his price, we subconsciously convince ourselves as well that the object is of inferior quality. This is even more true if you steal such an object, thereby expressing the feeling that you aren't prepared to pay even a cent for it.

The most important quality of such objects is the faith you have in them. The most poorly made materials are of tremendous value when you believe in them wholeheartedly. The most ancient and finest magical objects are useless if you doubt them even a little, making even the terrific bargain price you paid much too high.

Of course, magical tools received as gifts under unusual circumstances are the most valuable. For example, you help an unknown beggar out of a desperate situation and offer your hospitality. The next day, the beggar is gone, but has left behind a deck of cards covered with mysterious pictures. Such stories are often told by magicians and card readers among the gypsies. And if someone points out that the same cards can be bought at a nearby store—well that person should be told that the power of the cards is not a factor of their origins, but of their having been received as an unexpected payment for a good deed.

On Lending Your Deck

Since 1965, I have "surveyed" nineteen tarot readers for their opinions about lending their cards to other people.

Fifteen said they would never let anyone else use their cards, but only four of them could give logical reasons, such as the tendency people have to return used items bruised, battered, or with missing parts. Three others had simply been told by their teachers never to lend their cards to anyone. The remaining eight said the cards must always be in contact with their owners' own powers and vibrations. Four of these eight said this was an ancient occult law, while the other four referred to modern concepts like orgone, bio-electricity, magnetism, or the cosmic energy emanating from all beings.

Of the nineteen I questioned, fourteen recommended carrying the deck at all times in a cloth or leather pouch decorated with magical symbols, in order to imbue the cards fully with the owner's vibrations, thus making the cards more dependable and accurate. This practice is followed by many gypsy readers. Many also always wash their hands before removing the cards from their pouch.

The Power of Faith

One fact which no tarot reader argues is that the person who comes for a reading should have a strong trust in the cards. This trust or faith is as important as the cards themselves. The best cards available cannot do their work when

Figure 14. Modern tarot enthusiasts, like their predecesors in the 18th and 19th centuries, see the images as a window to the star worship of ancient ancestors. Illustration from The Primitive World, *by Court de Gebelin, Vol. 8, Paris, 1781.*

someone doubts them, while an ordinary deck of playing cards can give wonderful readings for the person who believes in them. Your own attitude will also have an effect on the person requesting a reading. You have to believe in what you are doing, in your cards and in what you say. Those who see tarot readings as a quick and easy way to make money fool no one but themselves.

The nature of human beings is to be honest, so we make poor and transparent liars. No matter what our words say, our bodies give hundreds of clues as to what we really mean. This is why experienced businesspeople like to shake the hands of people they are dealing with, or look deeply into their eyes, or use any other technique to notice whether there is any sign of discomfort, bad conscience or any other symptom of less than complete honesty. You cannot give tarot readings for long if you have no faith in what you are doing.

Your trust, combined with the atmosphere you create when you do a reading, will help your clients relax, drop their own attitudes of doubt, and open themselves to the images and messages of the tarot.

Chapter Eight

THE READER'S TABLE

YOU WILL WANT TO arrange a table or surface to do your readings. For some, a plain piece of beautiful cloth which doubles as a wrapping for the deck is enough. You can add incense, candles, crystals or other objects to make the table and room more conducive to the mood of a reading. Among the gypsies, many factors are considered when arranging a table.

One technique takes the four directions into consideration. The reader sits, slightly elevated, back to the north and face to the south (the sun) so that the client's back is toward the south. The south represents fire, always wanting and needing more matter to burn. It represents life, questions, expectation, burning desire, restlessness and impatience. From the north come the decisions of the gods, both the lucky and unlucky stars. The north represents reality and the earth with all its riches. The east, representing morning and spring is to the reader's left. The west representing evening and autumn is to the reader's right. Some tarot readers even lay a sword or dagger at the left of the table and a cup or goblet with water or wine in it at the right, to symbolize the elements air and water.

Three candles stand between reader and client, nearer to the client. They symbolize the client's questions and desires.

As you draw cards, lay them left to right, so that the person opposite sees them as reading from right to left. When laying out the Magic Wheel, place the first card at the south, directly in front of the questioner. Continue toward the right where the west and the goblet of fluid are. The person coming for a reading feels uncertain and insecure in some way, which causes a waning of energies. Evening approaches, and the only hope lies in entering the depths, the darkness, where the gods, the stars of wisdom which can help solve any problem can be found. The cards proceed toward the north, the earth and midnight, because wisdom lies in those depths. The circle continues toward the east, the dagger and the element of air. Finally the circle brings advice and new energies to the person waiting at the south, much as the sun brings new hope and energies from the east to all beings.

As you see, you can use your knowledge of alchemy, astrology, ancient religions, etc. to help you arrange and conduct your readings.

Creating an Atmosphere

You may want to create a special atmosphere in the room you use for readings, to help yourself and your clients enter into the right mood. You can use incense and candles, paintings, tapestries and/or crystals, as well as music.

Exotic surroundings can throw people a little off-balance, especially those who stoutly claim to have both feet planted firmly on the ground and no interest in magical nonsense. Their uncertainty in unfamiliar surroundings can help them step from their logical, rational world of ideas into the world of symbols and into their own subconscious. A reading done under these circumstances can be far more striking and make a much deeper impression.

Your behavior can also have a profound effect on your client. If you are open and direct, talking without embarrassment or hesitation about even very personal topics, your client will be more inclined to be open as well. If you speak in euphemisms or avoid "delicate" subjects, your reluctance will be felt and mirrored by your client. Remember that your task is to get the other person to reflect honestly on him- or herself.

Modern gypsy tarot readers who follow the ancient traditions pay strict attention to their manner of speaking, the lighting, the decoration of the room, mirrors and incense to create an inner readiness in themselves and their guests. The two people can then more readily establish the necessary rapport or energy field, much as a midwife and birthing mother do. When the two are tuned in, memories, intuitions and perceptions become more vivid and available, making the reading more far-reaching and effective.

Chapter Nine

HOW TO DO A READING

PLEASE REMEMBER THAT AMONG all the hundreds of books about tarot which have flooded the market since the early 1970s, you will not find any complete textbook in which you can look up exact answers to everything. The tarot contains seventy-eight cards with one hundred fifty-six possible meanings, depending on whether they are right-side up or inverted. In addition, each card is read in relation to the "basic card," the one drawn to represent the person asking the questions. If the questioner is represented by the Three of Cups, the cards drawn in response to the questions will be interpreted differently than if the questioner's basic card is the Magician.

Obviously, a tarot book can't cover all the possibilities, any more than a child's ABC book can begin to hint at what a great poet will be able to do with those letters. Your only recourse is to practice doing readings, and reflect on the meanings of the cards. Good readers say that the cards must speak directly to you, so that you could fill an entire book with your thoughts about just one of them.

I will describe here two of the many games you can use to help you discover the deeper meanings of the cards.

The Paths to Salvation

Lay the 22 Major Arcana in three rows as shown in Figure 15. Start with 1 (the Magician), and take every third card after it to form the first row. Start the second row with 2 (the Priestess), and the third row with 3 (the Empress). The Fool is not used since it can have either the number 0 or 22, and represents the person who stands at the beginning of the path, or the person who has missed it. These three rows now consist of the following cards:

1, 4, 7, 10, 13, 16, and 19;
2, 5, 8, 11, 14, 17 and 20;
and 3, 6, 9, 12, 15, 18 and 21.

They represent the three paths we can take toward higher consciousness.

The first is the way of the Magician, of Osiris or Vishnu. If we read from right to left, we see first the person who chooses this path by seeking the light of realization (19, the Sun). Then, although passing through Destruction (16,

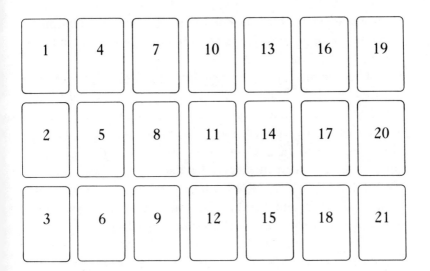

Figure 15. The Paths to Salvation layout.

the Tower) and Death (13), he or she recognizes that Fortune (10) is leading toward the goal. Conscious action is represented by 7 (the Chariot), and the ability to rule one's own world by 4 (the Emperor). The goal is the Magician, the one no longer bewildered by the confusing game in this colorful fairground of life.

The second path is the way of the High Priestess, of creation, rebirth, Brahma. Again reading from the right, we see the person on this path recognizing the world as a unified work, a divine creation (20, Judgement) and as the divine source of all cosmic forces (17, the Star). Temperance (14) results in mastery over natural energies, and in Strength (11) which grows when used in the service of cosmic balance and Justice (8). Fulfillment as either the Hierophant or Priestess is the ultimate goal.

The third path is the way of the Empress (3), or of Venus, the morning star, the fairy. It is the path neither of action nor of recognition of divine mercy, but of increased experience. It begins with the World (21), leads to a meeting with the forces of the night (18, the Moon) and its rather eerie master (15, the Devil). It leads through rigorous tests (12, the Hanged Man) to new wisdom (9, the Hermit) which makes good decisions possible. Finally you attain mastery over yourself and your world.

The Three Hexagrams

The hexagram, or six-pointed star, is an ancient symbol found in Indian religions, the Germanic runes, Jewish Cabbala and European and gypsy magic traditions.

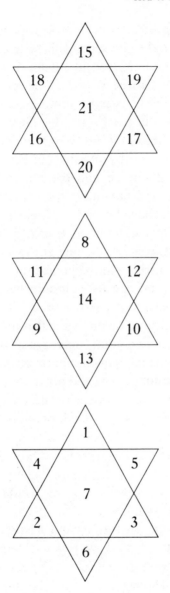

Figure 16. The Three Hexagrams layout.

When laying out the cards, we usually place the first hexagram at the right, the second at the left, and the third in the middle. As you can see in Figure 16, the first star is formed by placing 21 (the World) in the center, and building a downward pointing triangle around it. Judgement (20) comes directly under the World, the Sun (19) to the right above it and the Moon (18) to the left above it. The second triangle is constructed by placing the Star (17) below 19, the Tower (16) below 18 and the Devil (15) at the top. Each star is built in this manner, forming first the downward pointing triangle, then the upward pointing one.

In the downward pointing triangles, the card at the right represents the spirit, the one at the left represents the material, visible world, and the point represents the synthesis of the two. In the upward pointing triangles, the card at the right represents the passive or masochistic aspect of human nature, and the one at the left represents the active or sadistic aspect. The point, once again, is the synthesis— the ideal being who contains both aspects in equilibrium. In other words, the first triangle represents the creation, the world, and the second represents the creature living in it. The card at the center is the result of the interaction of both triangles.

In the first star or hexagram, the Sun (19) balances the Moon (18). This is the interplay of day and night, light and matter, conscious and subconscious. Understandably, they give rise to the Judgement (20), the image of eternal reincarnation, or creation. In the second triangle, the Star (17) reminds us what is ours if we follow cosmic laws, and the Tower (16) shows us our fate if we don't. Their synthesis is the Devil (15), whom we are doomed to misunderstand if we see him as the church describes him. He is really the satyr full of boundless energy and potency. He is the synthesis of all animal qualities, is master of the animal realm, but is still without knowledge of the difference between

good and evil. The card in the center is self-explanatory –
the eternal dance of the World results from the unification
of all cosmic forces and elements.

The second hexagram is that of the Adversary, the
great opponent of the Creator. According to gypsy and
wicca tradition, the devil helped humanity follow God's
great plan by forcing us to decide between good and evil,
putting us on the path toward becoming conscious beings.

The first triangle shows that, seen from the spiritual
aspect, the world is a test (12, the Hanged Man), while
from the material aspect, the world is a struggle in which
Strength prevails (11). Anyone who knows the world only
through this triangle sees it as an eternal dance of Death
(13). In this scenario, the passive person is like a leaf tossed
by the winds of the Wheel of Fortune's rapid spinning (10).
The active person sees no choice but to withdraw from this
vale of tears to become a Hermit (9) and reflect on Justice
(8), the cosmic balance. Everything is ultimately revealed as
maya, a trick of illusion, as we can interpret Temperance
(14).

In the third hexagram, the Priest (4) rules the world of
spirit and the Emperor (5) is rightful ruler over the world of
matter. A decision (6) is easier when both possibilities are as
clearcut and positive as these are. Beneath the Priest is the
Empress (3) – the worldly person who recognizes the power
of the divine and rules according to the moral and ethical
values which govern us. On the other side, the Priestess (2)
is below the Emperor – the realm of spirit serves the world.
The Chariot of victory (7), symbol of the conscious interaction of all forces, is at the center, while the Magician (1),
who can juggle and unify all aspects and all the other cards,
stands above it all.

The three hexagrams can also be seen as an explanation for the three candles often placed on the table of the
tarot reader. They symbolize the creator, the destroyer and

the "bringer of joy." This trinity has its roots in the Indian trimurti of Brahma the Creator, Shiva the Destroyer and Krishna the Savior. Krishna in this context is often seen as a divine showman or magician.

• • •

If you want to really learn the meanings of each card, the "language of the arcana," you should study each card, as well as other symbolic figures to familiarize yourself with the images. You may receive inspiration or instruction from others more knowledgeable than you, or you can draw your own tarot deck, as so many other people have done throughout the ages. You can copy designs from other decks, or design your own according to your own thoughts, perceptions, inspirations and dreams.

Remember also, that once you understand the cards well, the cards you lay for the past will contain the present, and the future as well, if you are able to read the signs.

One Parisian reader told me, "You can go to all the occult schools and read the most esoteric books on exotic magic, but you will surely find no definitive words, no basic truth which you could not have found by merely observing the cards and the people who work with them and know them well."

Portrait of the Client

One of the most basic and important skills of a good tarot reader is that of choosing the appropriate card to represent the person asking a question. This card helps the reader understand the client and what forces are motivating his or her actions. There are two common methods for selecting a card:

1) Mix the cards carefully. Some readers use only the 22 Major Arcana while some like to use the entire deck. Let your client cut the deck three times, and then either you or your client pick a card and lay it face down on the table. This will be the first card you interpret after the rest of the layout has been chosen.

2) The other most common method is to choose, according to your impressions and intuition, which of the sixteen "ruler" cards most closely represents your client. Usually the kings are taken for men, the queens for women, knights for youths and the pages for young women.

Your choice can be based on many factors, including the person's origins or profession, appearance or temperament. In ancient times, temperaments were classified into four types: sanguine, corresponding to air, spring and motion (Swords); choleric, corresponding to fire, summer and fiery action (Wands); melancholic, corresponding to earth, autumn and deep, solid, slow movement (Coins); and phlegmatic, corresponding to water, winter and peaceful or calm and flowing movement (Cups). Another old tradition teaches that Wands represent very fair people, Cups represent somewhat fair people. Swords represent dark people and Coins represent very dark or swarthy people.[1]

You may want to wash your hands before beginning to work with the cards. Always mix them carefully and let the person asking the questions cut the cards three times. Both of you should use your left hands when cutting the deck or choosing cards. After the cards have been mixed and cut, you can choose the card to represent the questioner, using one of the techniques described earlier.

You can choose the cards for the reading either by taking one from any part of the deck, and the ones next to it in sequence, or you can take each card separately from different parts of the deck by fanning the cards out on the table and selecting each one-by-one. You can lay the cards either face-down or face-up, but always be careful when turning them over not to alter the right-side up or inverted position of the cards.

Chapter 10

LAYOUT TECHNIQUES

BEFORE DESCRIBING SOME example layouts, I would like to emphasize that everything said in this section is only a suggestion, not a hard and fast rule to be memorized and blindly followed. There is no dogma or set philosophy to be learned before using the cards. By giving some examples, I hope merely to help you set your own imagination free to devise your own games and techniques. Perhaps you will also meet someone "by coincidence" who knows the tarot well and will share new ideas with you, and help you along. Such a meeting can be wonderful and informative, but remember that your own work with the cards is most important.

The Three Rows

One of the simplest techniques is to lay the cards in three rows of three cards each. I learned this as a child from my mother, and have since seen it used in many countries by many different tarot readers, including Walter Wegmüller and his circle of tarot-reading friends.

After choosing the card to represent the client, choose nine more cards, arranging them in three rows of three as shown in figure 17.

The top row represents the past, the middle represents the present and the bottom row represents the future. When interpreting the cards, start with the middle one in each row. It stands for the basic conditions of the entire situation and reflects the influence of what is shown in the preceding row. The card to the left, representing the negative forces, like conflicting desires, is read next, and the one to the right, representing the final outcome of the antithesis or interaction between the opposing forces is read last.

I will illustrate this technique with an example which you may want to lay out to look at yourself. Our client's card is the Two of Swords. He has two very well-developed and strong models of the world—ideals which he cannot bring into harmony. Perhaps he has a fancifully chivalrous philosophy resulting from his mother's romantic dreams, idealistic books etc., and then he trained to become a scientist in hope of experiencing incredible mental adventures. He is shocked to discover that his colleagues see their work as a means of putting food on their tables rather than as a means of delving into the mysteries of God and the world.

The cards for his past confirm this idea. In the center is the High Priestess (2), to the left is the Three of Wands, and to the right is the Four of Cups, inverted.

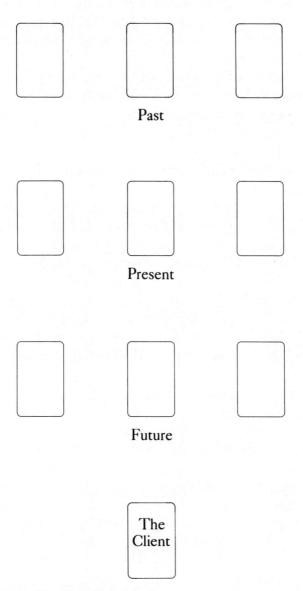

Figure 17. The Three Rows layout.

The moon goddess, the great mother, ruled his childhood and youth. She was probably his biological mother and her influence was most felt on the religious aspect of his life, helping shape his ideals.

When he tried to step out of that sphere of influence, he strove to "be a man," to put his ideals into practice. The outcome was a dismal failure. The Four of Cups is inverted. This represents his disappointment at discovering that his beautiful dreams just didn't mesh with reality as he experiences it. The models, ideals, and concepts of youth spill away and are lost.

The present is represented by the Tower (16) in the center, the Ace of Swords inverted at the left, and the Five of Coins at the left. Everything appears to crumble around him (Tower). His strong, well-educated mind works self-destructively. All the tremendous potential of his own energies (Ace of Swords) leads him downward, into the grave. This card expresses the despair in which his mind constantly forges new, heavy, black thoughts to chain him. It seems senseless to try to accomplish anything with noble motives.

The immediate outcome (the Five of Coins) seems positive—an unexpected opportunity to make some money quickly. Combined with the other cards, however, it can represent a dangerous trap. Someone who throws himself into money-making after being disappointed in achieving his higher spiritual ideals can become a more evil and repellant capitalist than someone who has been brought up believing that making money is the purpose of life.

The future contains the Four of Wands inverted in the center, the Queen of Cups to the left and the Seven of Coins to the right.

The Four of Wands reversed points to your client's state of total confusion regarding his potential in the realm of practical realities and activity. He stands before two conflicts, two dualities. After the destruction of his idealized world of Cups, he can throw himself fully into external activity, thereby being perceived by those around him as thoughtless and destructive, or he can shy away from that possibility, thereby placing his material existence in jeopardy. Either way, he can only fail, his failures on the material plane expressing his deep inner disappointment.

The Queen or Lady of Cups brings salvation. She is the female figure he will either meet, or whose true worth he will suddenly realize (if he already knows her) in the near future. She is in some ways similar to the High Priestess and will bring his mother's world back, but in a new form, with his childhood ideals modified to better fit into reality.

The outcome (Seven of Coins) is not only the ability to easily and imaginatively achieve economic success, but also to invest the winnings wisely again and again in the game of life – including in service to the ideals he holds dear.

Once a reading is completed, the client can ask three additional related questions or draw three more cards for clarification of certain points in the reading. He may only ask three, so that no more than thirteen cards are face-up on the table at any one time. Twelve represent the zodiac, and the thirteenth represents the sun.

The client in the above reading would like more information about the Lady of Cups, and the Ten of Swords is drawn. This is superb! His involvement with the woman indicated will result in his becoming able to maintain an overview of his mental powers and utilize them with awareness.

To clarify the Seven of Coins, the Chariot (7) is drawn. The message here is that he who steers his economic gains toward serving his highest ideals achieves his aim and possesses true good fortune.

The third question concerns the High Priestess, and the King of Coins is drawn inverted. Considering the rest of the reading, we can interpret this card as representing the client's father figure, whose influence was felt most through his absence. Whether he died early or was simply totally absorbed in his world of Coins, the father left his child's upbringing to the mother. The father's worldly, practical outlook could have provided a balance to the mother's religious idealistic model of the world. In the absence of that modifying influence, the boy's view of the world became weighted too heavily on the mother's side, resulting in his extremely strong revulsion toward the burdensome world of money and the material world which robbed him and his mother of his father.

With the arrival of the Lady of the Cups, he will be better able to find a balance between the two aspects and let go of the conflicts stemming from these childhood experiences.

The Magic Circle or Magic Wheel

Whether or not the word "tarot" is related to the word "rota," meaning wheel, symbols of movement and wandering or transformation are frequently found in the images. Walter Wegmüller often saw the wheel used as a tarot symbol among the gypsies of the Jura, and has used it as a decoration on each of the 78 cards, giving the deck some of its traditional gypsy flavor.

I was taught that the Magic Wheel must not be learned from books. You must either develop your own technique, or learn it from a real master of the tarot. You may not pass your knowledge of it on to anyone else, except, perhaps, to your own child or a beloved pupil, if you have one. While adhering to this teaching, I will present, as a basis for your own further experimentation, a simple "Tarot Ring."

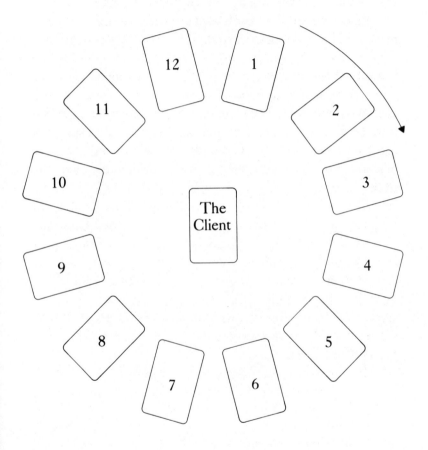

Figure 18. The Magic Wheel layout.

As always, first choose the basic card for the person requesting the reading, and place it in the center. As shown in figure 18, start at the top (in a noon position if you think of a clock) and lay twelve cards face down, moving in a clockwise direction around the card in the center.

Be careful to place each card as you have drawn it, so it remains heads-up or inverted. The top of the card will always be on the outside of the circle, so the cards at the bottom of the circle near you will appear upside down to you and right-side up to your client. For example, the Ace of Wands drawn inverted will look right-side up to you. You may need some practice to get used to this! Be especially careful to use the correct hand movement when turning over the cards to read them, to avoid accidentally changing their positions.

After the circle is laid out, your client asks a question. Begin at any one of the cards, and turn it over. Continue around the circle in a clockwise direction, turning over every third card, until four are face up. The first card you turned over represents the wishes and desires behind the question, the second represents the forces working in opposition to the situation, the third represents the forces which are supporting the questioner, and the fourth represents the probable outcome.

Two more questions can be answered using the same technique to turn over the cards until all twelve are face up.

The Tarot as an Oracle

You can ask the tarot for a clear "yes" or "no" answer to any question. Many readers reject this technique as the worst kind of superstition, for they feel that this practice is bound to lead its practitioners into total dependence and loss of free will.

The tarot is a tool for people who want to become aware of the myriad possibilities presented by the game of life, or for those who want to see images of the past, present and future and discover the correlation between them. Used this way, the tarot becomes a tool on our path toward ultimate understanding. We need to guard against using the tarot when we are stuck at an apparent dead-end, without also seeking causes and deeper understanding. With that in mind, you can use the following two methods of arriving at a "yes" or "no" answer.

Some readers use only the 22 Major Arcana for this first game, while others use the entire deck. Whichever you choose, allow the person you are reading for to cut the deck three times with the left hand. Draw a single card from the deck. A card with an uneven (male) number means "yes," and one with an even number (female) means "no." The knights and kings are male, while the queens and pages are female. As mentioned earlier, in some decks the pages are depicted as princesses.

In the second game, you draw seven cards and lay them face up. If the majority of them are right-side up, the answer is "yes." If the majority are inverted, the answer is "no." Instead of just answering a question, this method also provides deeper insights into the situation at hand.

The middle card in the seven card layout tells you why you have gotten this particular answer. The three cards to the left contain hints as to the consequences of acting on this answer.

The seven card spread can also be read in another way. The cards to the right of center indicate the basis for the

Figure 19. Using a seven card layout to find an answer to a question.

answer received as well as which favorable forces are present. The cards to the left of center reveal the consequences of not following the tarot's advice.

Suppose a man asks the cards, "Should I take the better paying position which has been offered to me?" You draw seven cards, five of which stand upright. The answer is a clear "yes."

Now we can look deeper. Figure 19 shows the cards that our man picked. The card in the middle is the Magician (1). In this case, it represents the questioner's basic motivation. Rather than seeking position or financial gain, he is seeking knowledge about himself and the world around him. He is following his creative urge to play life's game. Having mastered one set of tasks, he is eager to explore his abilities and possibilities by embarking on a new adventure. He is like the carnival magician who, having shown the people in one area the best of his conjuring, must move to a new audience before his tricks begin to appear stale. If both magician and audience are wise, the finest gift—the gift of love—will also be shared. When the magician moves on to another audience, he gains new perspectives, as well as a certain freshness, by doing the same tricks for new eyes.

The Queen of Cups is to the right of the Magician, along with the Page of Swords inverted, and the Ace of Wands. Your client hopes that a change in career and the resulting adventure will make the woman in his life happy. He lives for her, and she sees living with him as the fulfillment of some divine plan. She has more to offer than he could ever imagine.

The powerful standing Ace of Wands indicates that the change, or the courage he needs to make it, will bring his masculine energies to a new peak.

The Page of Swords stands on his head—the change will bring with it one disadvantage. He will never achieve mastery in his present occupation. If, despite his desire for change, he were to remain in his present position, he could become better and better at it. It would cease to be just a job, and grow to be a calling. He would no longer be just a worker with his staff, but would become an invincible fencer with his sword, a master. His job could become a creative, growing, ever-changing art.

To the Magician's left are the Priestess, the Page of Cups inverted, and the Empress. If your client doesn't follow the tarot's advice, but decides to stay put and develop his present skills, he will meet with great success.

The Priestess and Empress indicate he will be admired and respected by all people—those who value material success as well as those who recognize the material as an external manifestation of his inner growth and development.

The Page of Cups stands on his head, spilling out the holy contents of his cup. If your client does not follow the tarot's advice, his professional success will be overshadowed by his gradual loss of the woman who is more important to him than anything else. His only real desire is to live happily with her and have time and energy to spend with her. His work isn't a means of gaining new abilities and knowledge, but a means of obtaining stimulation or new ideas to bring home—his homecoming becomes an occasion for joy, and the two continue to delight in each other and find their real fulfillment in their love.

Some people stay in the same jobs all their lives and, to avoid boredom, change their friends and/or spouses every few years. This client is not one of them. He expects and will probably find a fountain of youth in his new job. The longer he is with the same woman, the more she can and will give him. However, for this very reason, he feels inferior to her and is afraid he'll be unable to receive and appreciate her gifts if he slowly becomes stale, old, and exhausted by the monotony of engaging in the same tasks day in and day out. The tarot advises him clearly to take the new position.

NOTES

Part One: The World of the Gypsies

1. Theophrastus Paracelsus, *Collected Works*, edited by B. Aschner (Jena, 1926–1932), Vol. 4, pp. 327–331.

2. Ibid., p. 339.

3. Compare Eliphas Lévi, *Key of the Mysteries* (York Beach, ME: Samuel Weiser, 1970; and London: Rider, 1959).

4. J. V. Andreae, *Fama fraternitatis* (1614), referred to in *The True and Invisible Rosicrucian Order*, by Paul Foster Case (York Beach, ME: Samuel Weiser, 1985).

5. Hargrave Jennings, *The Rosicrucians, Their Rites and Mysteries* (Ayer Company Publishing, 1976; reprint of 1907 edition).

6. A. C. Bhaktivedanta Prabhupada, *Teachings of Lord Chaitanya* (New York, 1972), p. 166.

7. N. Douglas, *Tantra Yoga* (New Delhi, 1971), p. 13.

8. C. G. Leland, *Gipsy Sorcery* (London: T. Fischer Unwin, 1891).

9. Among the "Jena" from western and central Switzerland, the words *scharotl, schariotl,* and *rotu* are more usual.

10. W. Starkie, *Auf Zigeunerspuren* (Munich: 1957), p. 305.

11. W. A. Chatto, *Facts and Speculations on the Origin and History of Playing Cards* (London, .1848).

12. Lama Anagarika Govinda, *Foundations of Tibetan Mysticism* (York Beach, ME: Samuel Weiser, 1969; and London: Rider, 1960), p. 161.

13. J. D. Blakeley, *The Mystical Tower of the Tarot* (London: 1974), p. 11.

14. M. Mayhofer, *Kurzgefasstes etymologisches Worterbuch des Altindischen* (Heidelberg, 1974), Vol. 3, p. 26f.

15. Compare R. L. Turner, *A Comparative Dictionary of the Indo-Aryan Languages* (London, 1966), p. 609.

16. J. Pokorny, *Indogermanisches etymologisches Worterbuch* (Bern, 1959), Vol. 1, p. 512.

17. J. G. I. Breitkopf, *Versuch den Ursprung der Spielkarten . . . Zu erforschen* (Leipzig, 1784), Vol. 1, p. 114.

18. A. Elyseeff, in *Journal of Gypsy Lore Society* (Edinburgh, 1890); C. G. Leland, *Gipsy Sorcery,* 253f; S. Golowin, *Zigeunermagie im Alpenland* (Frauenfeld, 1972), p. 33ff.

19. Dr. Georg Stempowski, orally, during his stay in Bern as a refugee in 1955.

20. T. Benfey, *Pantschatantra* (Leipzig, 1859), Vol. 2, p. 48ff. Modern "fantastical realists" use this fairy tale as a "memory" of a highly developed civilization in times of pre-history, which possessed flying machines. Compare with W. R. Drake, *Spacemen in the East* (London, 1973).

21. H. Mode and S. Wolffling, *Gypsies* (Leipzig, 1968), p. 93ff.

22. M. Voriskova, *Singende Geigen, Zigeunermarchen* (Zurich, 1968), p. 9ff.

23. J. Burke, *Dr. Terror's House of Horror* (Munich, 1966), p. 11.

24. H. P. Blavatsky, *The Secret Doctrine* (Wheaton, IL: Theosophical Publishing House, 1977; reprint of 1888 edition).

25. Compare the systems of Blavatsky, A. Besant, F. Hartmann, Rudolf Steiner, M. Heindel and H. E. Mieers, *Lexikon des Geheimwissens* (Freiburg, 1970), p. 326f; compare also, T. Leary, *The Seven Tongues of God,* first appeared in *Psychedelic Review,* 1964; also T. Leary, *The Politics of Ecstasy* (New York, 1968).

26. Compare A. Danielou, *The Gods of India* (Rochester, VT: Inner Traditions, 1985). Also in other myths, the number 7 occurs frequently: there are supposedly 21 or 49 (7 x 7) "Maruts"; there are 7 or 14 forms of fairies or Apsaras, etc.

Part Two: The Meanings of the Cards

1. Compare *The Siva Purana* (Delhi, 1970), Vols. 1–4. The Indian scriptures speak repeatedly of the four (originally of equal worth) life goals.

2. In Tessin, Como, Mantua (southern Switzerland and northern Italy) the word "Tarock" in the dialects spoken means simply "stick." Compare J. Coromina, *Diccionario de la lengua castellana* (Bern, 1954), Vol. 3, p. 496 and Vol. 4, p. 395.

3. Until this day, the description of gypsy occult history is influenced by J. A. Vaillant, *Les Romes* (Paris, 1857).

4. Compare Papus, *ABC illustre d'occultisme* (Paris, 1972), p. 331ff; and Papus, *The Tarot of the Bohemians* (North Hollywood, CA: Wilshire, 19).

5. "Without a [human] body, no one attains a human being's highest goal; this is why one should care for the body as if it were a treasure, and do good works with it." *(Tr.)* D. *Pretakalpa* of the *Garuda-Purana*, E. Abegg (Berlin, 1956), p. 215.

6. Theophrastus Paracelsus, *Collected Works*, edited by B. Aschner (Jena, 1926–1932), Vol. 4, pp. 894f.

7. J. Richepin, *Miarka* (Paris, 1888), pp. 42ff.

8. *The Ananga ranga of Kalyana malla*, p. 30f.

9. Eliphas Lévi, *The History of Magic* (York Beach, ME: Samuel Weiser, 1970; and London: Rider, 1969).

10. W. Brown, *How to Tell Fortunes with Cards* (New York, 1965), p. 7. "It is to the gypsies one must go to learn the innermost secrets of cartomancy." K. Martin, *The Complete Gypsy Fortune-Teller* (New York: Berkley Books, 1972), p. 13.

11. C. P. Hargrave, *A History of Playing Cards* (New York: Dover, 1966), p. 27.

12. A. Danielou, *The Gods of India* (Rochester, VT: Inner Traditions, 1985).

13. Papus, *Le tarot divinatoire* (Paris, 1965), p. 162ff.

14. W. Starkie, *Auf Zigeunerspuren* (Munich, 1957), p. 306f; compare especially Court de Gébelin, *The Primitive World* (Paris, 1781).

15. Starkie, *Auf Zigeunerspuren*, pp. 259f.

16. Court de Gébelin, *The Primitive World*, p. 378; J. G. I. Breitkopf, *Versuch den Ursprung der Spielkarten . . . Zu erforschen* (Leipzig, 1784), p. 20.

17. A. Douglas, *The Tarot* (Baltimore: Penguin Books, 1974), p. 108.

18. Compare G. Moakley, *The Tarot Cards Painted by Bembo* (New York, 1966); G. Mandel, *I Tarocchi dei Visconti* (Bergamo, 1974).

19. A. Danielou, *The Gods of India*. "Madhava," one of Vishnu-Krishna's most important names, is sometimes translated as meaning "the one filled with Madhu, Soma (the intoxicating drink)."

20. W. Eidlitz, *Der Sinn des Lebens, Der indische Weg* (Olten, 1974), pp. 158f.

21. A. Douglas, *The Tarot*, p. 85.

22. A. Danielou, *The Gods of India*, pp. 339f.

23. Compare *The Kamasutra of Vatsyayana*, pp. 56ff.

Part Three: How to Read the Cards

1. R. G. Torrens, *The Golden Dawn, The Inner Teachings* (York Beach, ME: Samuel Weiser, 1973), p. 163.